NEW SERIES • VOLUME XX

Essays in
English and American
Language and Literature

Rodopi

1979

NORMAN MAILER'S NOVELS

by

Sandy Cohen

1979

© Editions Rodopi N.V., Amsterdam 1979
Printed in the Netherlands
ISBN: 90–6203–912–X

For K.C. and K.C.

CONTENTS

Chapter One: Norman Mailer

in Context

The earliest American writers were not Americans. They were not born in America either physically or spiritually. They belonged to, and thought of themselves as being born in the Old, blighted, World. And yet they also thought of themselves as being born again into the New, salubrious, World. They viewed history as teleological, by and large. They viewed its purpose as promise and its promise as approaching fulfillment. Writers as separated in temperament and time as William Bradford and Thomas Paine wrote of man's coming personal and social perfection. From the Plymouth Fathers to Natty Bumpo, the literary heroes that American writers created were "civilizers" of the rough and raw Land of Potential. And for the next few generations of writers the land was the Book of God. They, William Cullen Bryant, Ralph Waldo Emerson, Henry David Thoreau and the like, were there to read that book, interpret it, urge its message, and fulfill its prophecy.

By the end of the nineteenth century nearly all of these idealists were gone. Beginning with the ethical idealists and realists of the early nineteenth century and continuing through the disillusionists of this century, the stories the story-tellers told were quite different. From Hawthorne to Faulkner the vision

of a lost, mislaid, or damaged Eden emerged and sharpened. The
history, and, subsequently, the future, of the United States was
seen as one of tragic decline. At first, in writers such as Hawthorne and Melville, the vision was of a decline from a golden age.
Gradually, as in Farrell and Faulkner, the vision became one of
decay from an already spoiled stock. This original blight was
seen variously as displacement, slavery, religious zeal, or, quite
simplistically, Original Sin. The element of apocalypse was added
to this vision when the bombs dropped over Nagasaki and Hiroshima.

What went wrong? This was a major theme of the American
writers of the post war, or Norman Mailer's generation. For the
majority, Mailer included, the answer was not that the destructive
forces of history had finally caught up with themselves. To these
writers, history itself was rendered as purposeless because it
slouched toward a total, absolute, and unavoidable destruction.
All that was left, it would seem, was to contemplate whether this
fate of humanity's were man-made, random, or Purposeful. But whatever choice the writers of Mailer's generation made, they maintained
that it did not matter anyway, for the end results were the same;
both past and present were pointless.

Thus, with no belief in historical continuity, all acts, all
interests, became for these writers equivalent. For example, as
Robert Alter has pointed out,[1] the fire bombing of Dresden, in
Kurt Vonnegut Jr.'s Slaughterhouse Five, became exactly equal to
the murders at Auschwitz. On the other end of the scale, as in

Pynchon's Gravity's Rainbow, trivia were elevated to the level of significance.

> If history is no longer a realm of concatenation, if there are no necessary connections among discrete events and no possibility of a hierarchy of materials ranged along some chain of fantasies, any crotchety hobbyistic interest, any technical fascination with the rendering of odd trivia, can be pursued by the novelist as legitimately as the movement of supposedly "significant" actions. The end of history, in other words, is a writer's license for self indulgence. . . . [2]

and

> Man, at least in his political guise, is equally vile everywhere, whether he is a Nazi, an American, or a Soviet Russian, and so Dresden and Hiroshima are, quite without qualification, the exact equivalent of Auschwitz and Dachau.[3]

In other words, existence, for these writers, did not become simply separate from essence; essence disappeared. Nothing was left but wish-fulfillment.

Norman Mailer began his literary career shortly before these post war ideas began to be fully expressed in fiction. In fact, it was his first published novel, The Naked and the Dead, that in some measure helped to bring these ideas to the forefront in American letters. It was not until his second and subsequent novels that he fully addressed these new and thoroughly uncomfortable themes.

While the social theories presented in The Naked and the Dead were of the vanguard, the style of the novel harked back to the large, panoramic books of John Dos Passos, James T. Farrell, John Steinbeck, and other writers of American social realism. The combination of new wine in an old bottle was a happy one for Mailer; The Naked and the Dead was an overwhelmingly successful book with critics and public alike. It brought the very young author international fame, financial reward, and a great amount of scholarly attention. By examining the lives of various soldiers from all strata of American society, soldiers based heavily upon models with whom the author had served during World War II, Mailer analysed the varied, complex, interwoven, and transmuting economic, social, and, especially, political forces he observed building around him. For Mailer, these forces threatened the end of individual autonomy and human compassion.

In the years since writing The Naked and the Dead, Mailer has remained an astute political observer. His special concern has been the effect of politics and society upon the individual. Much of his fiction, and nonfiction as well, has dealt with the immediate and continuing effects of political and social power in its varied forms upon personal destiny and national custom. In the two novels that followed The Naked and the Dead, Barbary Shore and The Deer Park, Mailer explored what he considered the sources of post-war American mores, and their subsequent effects upon individuals. In Barbary Shore, he maintained that the failure of the Russian Revolution, especially the defeat and murder of Trotsky, acted as a catalyst

to the ruin of the socialist movement in America by what Mailer
called the fascists of the growing American bureaucracy. In
The Deer Park, Mailer presented a microcosm of the extremely
influential American motion picture industry. His major argument
was that this industry engendered an illusory moral code while
its members, and much of America as well, lived a grotesque perversion of it.

By the time he wrote his fourth and fifth novels, An American
Dream and Why Are We In Vietnam?, Mailer, like so many of his
American contemporaries, such as Philip Roth, Gore Vidal and others
already alluded to, was as devoted, or more so, to the indulgence
of private fantasies as he was to the broader questions of national
destiny. Indeed, in these two novels, national destiny and private
fantasy are combined in a highly arbitrary eschatology. As in the
novels of J.P. Donleavy, Vonnegut, Pynchon, Barthelme, Joseph Heller,
and others, Mailer, taking his cue perhaps from the "new" archeologists,
has maintained in his latest novels that mankind is now known not by
its Great Works but by its droppings. Pity the shade of Matthew Arnold:
gone, say these post war writers, are the high old days of Culture,
and the literary artist's efforts to espouse it. It is no wonder that
all the protagonists of Mailer's last two novels (Steven Rojack
of An American Dream and D.J. Jethroe of Why Are We In Vietnam?)
can manage is mere survival at worst, and personal gratification
at best. They can neither flourish nor achieve anything of lasting
value. And what is even more important, they have no desire to.

Their world is far removed from either flourishing or historical
progression. They cannot even acquire mastery over themselves.

Such is Norman Mailer's public vision of America. His private
image is not far removed. Since the popular success of The Naked
and the Dead, he has striven to attain the dual and clashing image
of the man of letters and the celebrity. In his book Advertisements
for Myself, Mailer baldly asserted that he was out to win the uneasy
crown that Ernest Hemingway wore: In the following years Mailer
learned how to box from the light-heavyweight champion of the world,
became involved in public brawls and abusive verbal debates, was
sometimes arrested for drunk and disorderly conduct, was committed
briefly to the psychiatric ward of a hospital after stabbing his
second wife, ran for mayor of New York City, became involved for
a while in the Vietnam anti-war movement, joined various voguish
causes, and even made the journalists' requisite pilgrimage to Plains,
Georgia after Jimmy Carter won the Presidential nomination, all in
the name of celebrity. Even ten or fifteen years after writing
Advertisements for Myself, Mailer continued to admit in such essays
of self-revelation and confession as The Prisoner of Sex and Existential
Errands his conscious cultivation of the controversial and his desire
to be thought of as the best American writer of his generation, the
heavyweight champion of literature.

In the pursuit of this personal obsession for recognition, Mailer
has written a great amount of journalism. These transitory works
sometimes illuminate the political and social observations of his
more important works. In such journalistic books as Of a Fire on

the Moon and Miami and the Seige of Chicago, Mailer has observed
and written about the fads, movements, political and sporting
events, and scientific endeavors which have helped to shape not
only his own philosophy, but much or America's philosophy as well.
In these reportings, which include major American political conventions, world heavyweight championship fights, the first landing
of men on the moon, the anti-Vietnam war march on Washington, and
the women's liberation movement, Mailer has tried not only to observe
from a distance but to participate, to do battle, as it were. This
need of his to be a part of the actions he narrates might be Mailer's
attempt to recapture that feeling of involement in world-shaping
forces that gave him his first success in The Naked and the Dead,
but may nevertheless have hurt his writing much more than even he
realizes.

Mailer himself has admitted many times the damage his ego may
have caused his alter-egos. Sometimes in the process of trying
to rescue that reputation as a literary artist he gained with The
Naked and the Dead, Mailer has gone astray. For example, in his
quest to prove his worth as a serious contender for Hemingway's
Crown of Literary Celebrity, Mailer has published a collection of
poetry, Deaths for the Ladies and Other Disasters. This book only
served to hurt its author's reputation with those very few who have
read it. Mailer has even gone so far away from his literary strong-
points as to have made a few amateur motion pictures. These, too,
have failed to win either the critical acclaim or the public acceptance he would have wanted, and have caused many critics to take less seriously

his more serious artistic endeavours. During the early years of his career, when he was most trying to imitate Ernest Hemingway, Mailer even made a recording about bullfighting. Luckily, it received even less attention than his motion pictures.

And so, through all the swagger and bravado, through all the mis-steps and false starts, what has Norman Mailer really done? What has he accomplished as a writer? It is fair to say that so far Norman Mailer has had his most success as a recorder of, and speculator about, the events and pressures that have helped to shape America's policies and living styles in the post World War II years. For first and foremost, Mailer's fictional genre has been the novel of ideas. And his non-fictional essays have likewise been creative forays into the world of contemporary ideas. Norman Mailer has helped us to understand the effect of war and revolution upon society and the individual, and the relationship between reality and fantasy, both private and public. It is also fair to say that his notions about those events and pressures, in turn, have helped greatly to shape his writing. Perhaps too greatly. Life does have a way of imitating art.

Whether these ideas are good, or true, is debatable. Whether they are lasting is unanswerable. What they are, however, and have always been, are provocative; that nobody can deny.

Notes: Chapter One

[1]Robert Alter, "The New American Novel," Commentary 60 (November, 1975).

[2]Alter, p.49.

[3]Alter, p.46.

Chapter II

The Naked and the Dead

During World War II, Norman Mailer served with the United
States 112 Cavalry, out of San Antonio, Texas. As he relates in
Advertisements for Myself,

> I may as well confess that by December 8th or
> 9th of 1941, in the forty-eight hours after Pearl
> Harbor, while worthy men were wondering where they
> could be of aid to the war effort, and practical
> young men were deciding which branch of the service
> was the surest of landing a safe commission, I was
> worrying darkly whether it would be more likely that
> a great war novel would be written about Europe or
> the Pacific.[1]

Mailer's military outfit was sent to the Pacific. His war experiences
there led directly to the writing of The Naked and the Dead. It is
the story of a fictional campaign near the end of the war to capture
the Japanese held island of Anapopei by the 460th Infantry of the
U.S. Army. In the course of telling the story of that campaign
through the eyes of the officers and enlisted men, Mailer portrayed
his conception of the power structure of the Army. By the use of
digression and allusion he argued that the power structure portrayed
was likewise his conception of the power structure of America's,
and, in various degrees, the world's, government. The use of war to
picture the power system was effective, for it clearly illustrated

Mailer's idea that the entire framework was then in flux, and that change was accompanied by great social and ideological conflict.

It was Mailer's belief that American state capitalism, as he saw it working, was the product of an unnatural coupling of business and government. According to Mailer, as the bureaucracies which would eventually control state capitalism began to grow, they acquired power once held by the individual. The individual, in turn, lost both his individuality and his personal consequence. This process Mailer argued through his portrayal of the lives of various members of the lower ranks of the Infantry, and in the conflicts between General Cummings, the symbol of the old power structure, Lieutenant Hearn, the representation of the old liberal opposition, and Major Dallison, the prototype of the new, aimless bureaucracy. To Mailer, this transfer of power from the individual to the bureau had causes and consequences which were political, psychological, metaphysical, and economic. These causes and consequences he speculates about in his character portrayals and plot conflicts of The Naked and the Dead.

Mailer believed that even though during the war a very few men such as General Cummings might be able to amass what seemed at first like great personal power, that power was really a house of cards; it would collapse as soon as its reasons for being disappeared. Once the power these men had gained fell in with the end of the war, the vacuum created would be filled by the growing bureaucracy of which Major Dallison was such an apt representative. In the story of the general, especially as it is told in the conflict

between him and Lieutenant Hearn, Mailer portrayed the rise and
fall of one of the last of the men who had even an illusion of
personal power.

Cummings himself is an apt symbol of the old-style power
broker. He is a man with the ability to use all situations to
his advantage, first by controlling his emotions, and second by using
the uncontrolled emotions of others as a force against them. For
example, in rejecting racial or class hatred unless it could be
used to gain and control others, Cummings says,

> "I've known men who've used filth until it became a
> high art. Statesmen, politicos, they did it for a
> purpose, and their flesh probably crawled. You can
> indulge your righteous rage but the things it comes out
> of are pretty cheap. The trick is to make yourself
> the instrument of your own policy. Whether you like
> it or not, that's the highest effectiveness man has
> achieved."[2]

Cummings feels that as a professed and cynical reactionary (he
describes himself as the "lord of [a] little abbey . . . waiting
for the renaissance of new power."), he is in a good position to
amass great personal power after the war. Cummings feels that he
is living in an incipient reactionary age. But he can achieve his
goal, he thinks, only if he can continue to control with absolute
authority the men below him and thus keep them working for him
effectively. He reasons that "the individual soldier . . . is a
more effective soldier the poorer his standard of living has been

in the past," and that "if you're fighting in the defense of your
own soil, then perhaps you're a little more effective." There is
one problem, however. He knows that his soldiers are presently
too taken with the idea of democracy to be effective subordinates.
As he explains to his aide, Robert Hearn, this idea must be elimi-
nated from the minds of those below him before he and the people
like him can begin to gain complete control.

> "They have an exaggerated idea of the rights due
> themselves as individuals and no idea at all of
> the rights due others. It's the reverse of the
> peasant, and I'll tell you right now it's the
> peasant who makes the soldier."
>
> "So what you've got to do is break them down,"
> Hearn said.
>
> "Exactly. Break them down. Every time an en-
> listed man sees an officer get an extra privilege,
> it breaks him down a little more."
>
> "I don't see that. It seems to me they'd hate
> you more."
>
> "They do. But they also fear us more. I don't
> care what kind of man you give me, if I have him
> long enough I'll make him afraid." [p. 175]

This idea is the foundation of what Cummings calls the "fear ladder."
As he puts it, "The Army functions best when you're frightened of the

man above you, and contemptuous of your subordinates." Mailer put

it even more succinctly in Existential Errands: "external manipulation

is authority." That in the end General Cummings loses his ability

to manipulate, and that Sergeant Croft, Lieutenant Hearn, and every-

one else in the novel are similarly defeated, is a vivid reminder

of Mailer's premise that in modern society the ability of anyone

to sustain personal power for even a short time is virtually im-

possible.

General Cummings mistakenly believes that if one could control

men during war, one could control them in exactly the same manner

once the war is over. The reason for his misjudgment is his mistaken

notion that the war is a "power concentration." He puts it this way:

> "I like to call it a process of historical energy.
> There are countries which have latent powers, latent
> resources, they are full of potential energy, so to
> speak. And there are great concepts which can unlock
> that, express it. As kinetic energy a country is or-
> ganization, co-ordinated effort, your epiphet, fascism.
> . . . Historically the purpose of this war is to
> translate America's potential into kinetic energy. The
> concept of fascism, far sounder than communism if you
> consider it, for it's grounded firmly in men's actual
> natures, merely started in the wrong country, in a
> country which did not have enough intrinsic potential
> power to develop completely. In Germany with that basic
> frustration of limited physical means there were bound

to be excesses. . . . America is going to absorb that
dream, it's in the business of doing it now. When
you've created power, materials, armies, they don't
wither of their own accord. Our vacuum as a nation is
filled with released power, and I can tell you that we're
out of the backwaters of history now. . . . For the past
century the entire historical process has been working
toward greater and greater concentration of power.
Physical power for this century, an extension of our
universe, and a political organization to make it possible. Your men of power in America, I can tell you,
are becoming conscious of their real aims for the first time
in our history. Watch. After the war our foreign pol-
icy is going to be far more naked, far less hypocritical
than it has ever been. We're no longer going to cover
our eyes with our left hand while our right is extending
an imperialistic paw." [pp. 321-322]

The main reason the general misreads history and the energy that
history is generating, Mailer implies, is that Cummings really does
not understand his own motives. According to his creator, the origin
of the power urges of Cummings and the social class he represents is
in his physical make-up. One cannot help noticing the word "latent"
in the general's explanation of his power system. Mailer goes to great
lengths to portray Cummings's background and to track the developement
of his ideas. This developement is traced in a digression which Mailer
calls "The Time Machine: General Cummings, A Particularly American

Statement." Mailer proposes in this digression that Cummings'
desire to create, control, and crush was fostered in part by the conflict between his mother, who insisted that he sew, paint, and read
such books as Ivanhoe, Oliver Twist and Little Lord Fauntleroy, and
his father, who violently opposed his son's engaging in such "womanly"
pastimes. His father finally shipped him off to military school,
and then to West Point. There the young future general's desires
for artistic creation were warped into desires for personal power
and domination over other men. He came out of the First World War
with the rank of first lieutenant, and with a chance, if he proceeded
correctly, to move high up in rank. With good fortune, and the help
of his wife, he does. All this time his lovemaking mirrors his
craving for power, for it is Mailer's contention that one's social
interactions are reflected in one's sexual activity. Thus, Mailer
says of the general and his wife,

> Their lovemaking is fantastic for a time:
>
> He must subdue her, absorb her, rip her apart
>
> And consume her. [p.415]

But later,

> he fights out battles with himself upon her
>
> body, and sometimes he withers in her. [p.416]

As Cummings begins to gain in rank he finds that his lack of formal
knowledge is beginning to hinder his growth in power so he begins to
read books of philosophy, political science, sociology, psychology,
history, literature and art. "He absorbs it and immediately trans-
mutes it into something else, satisfies the dominant warp in his
mind." [p. 420].

As his knowledge grows, Cummings realizes that he must broaden his base of power. He gets the opportunity to do so when he is sent officially to Paris to start an American subsidy of Leeway Chemicals, his brother-in-law's company. Here Mailer suggests the interlocking directory between business, military, and government organizations. But while on a side trip to Rome to perform some nebulous diplomatic mission, he gets drunk in a bar and picked up by a man. Cummings is led to an alley where the man's assistants are hiding. The assistants beat up Cummings and steal his wallet. From this episode Cummings realizes that his quest for domination and for personal power over men is in reality a latent homosexual impulse. Cummings takes the memory of this incident as a warning to himself, and decides henceforth to divert all of his energy into seeking to understand and to amass social, political, military and economic power. He sees the upcoming war as a good way to become a general. But even then he is thinking further ahead. He decides not to commit himself politically yet, but to keep his eyes open. He controls his latent homosexuality, yet it continues to dominate his mode of thought. It adds to his ultimate loss of power. For example, because of it he misjudges the psychology of his troops, thinking that if they sit long enough, they will, like him, attack of their own volition. Instead, they become lethargic. To relieve his feelings of personal impotence over this public failure, the general goes out to an artillery placement and fires one of the big Howitzer cannons. When he gets back to his tent he takes out his private journal. He describes the big gun not as the expected phallic symbol, but

as a symbolic vagina. He writes in his journal that he believes
men are no longer discrete from the machine. He thinks of the shell
of the Howitzer as the phallus and of the arc it describes in the
air as representing anything from the "form of all cultures," to
the curve "of a man or woman's breast," or the influence of mortality
and culture. At this point, however, he stops writing, deciding
that he is merely playing with words that mean nothing. As he says,
"It has been too pat, too simple. There was order but he could not
reduce it to the form of a single curve. Things eluded him." Implied is the idea that even with a society built upon Cummings'
terms, some individuals can get by unnoticed if the individual pos-
sesses the requisites for personal power and autonomy. This implication
Mailer will explore not only in this book, but for the rest of his
career.

Implied also is the idea that because of the complexity of post
war society, no one person could possibly gain control. Mailer suggests this idea completely in his descriptions of Cummings' pre-war
dealings during the Leeway Chemical episode. As the general explains
it to Hearn, the new power structure would be so complex that should
anyone be clever enough to control it, they would have to create a
whole new moral code in order to do so. Cummings envisions such a
code and relates it to Hearn.

> "The only morality of the future is a power morality,
> and a man who cannot find his adjustment to it is
> doomed. There is one thing about power. It can flow
> only from the top down. When there are little surges

of resistance at the middle levels, it merely calls

for more power to be directed downward, to burn it

out. [And] you can consider the Army . . . as a

preview of the future." [pp. 323-324]

Through General Cummings once again, Mailer goes on to surmise that

there are even metaphysical implications to his power system.

"There's that popular misconception of man as some-

thing between a brute and an angel. Actually, man

is in transit between brute and God."

"Man's deepest urge is omnipotence?"

"Yes. It's not religion, that's obvious, it's

not love, it's not spirituality, those are all sops

along the way, benefits we devise for ourselves

when the limitations of our existence turn us away

from the other dream. To achieve God." [p.323]

Even after he is defeated at the end of the book, Cummings still

dreams that a society such as he has outlined to Hearn is possible.

Thus, he muses,

There were few Americans who would understand

the contradictions of the period to come. The route

to control could best masquerade under a conservative

liberalism. The reactionaries and isolationists would

miss the bell, cause almost as much annoyance as they

were worth. Cummings shrugged. If he had another op-

portunity he would make better use of it. What frus-

tration! To know so much and be hog-tied. [p. 718]

In order to speculate about what would happen to individuals
were such a system as Cummings envisions to come about, Mailer
created a small-scale version of it in the I and R platoon which,
in the absence of a lieutenant, is under the control of Sergeant
Croft. Without the general's learning and intellect, Sergeant
Croft is a lower class version of Cummings' power manipulator.
Mailer traces the reasons Croft became a manipulator in a "Time
Machine" episode on him, called "The Hunger." In it, Mailer says
that the foundation for the persoanal power from which Croft de-
rives his ability to handle others comes from his father, who taught
him "never to be beaten in anything." An unfaithful wife later
taught Croft through experience the same maxim which General
Cummings arrived at intellectually: that the first rule in gaining
and keeping personal power is to trust only in oneself.

Certainly his background has left a cruel and vicious edge to
Croft's personality. Two examples will illustrate. The first involves an incident in which his platoon meets and defeats a small
Japanese patrol, thanks to Croft's personal, or rather, impersonal
courage. When the firing stops, Red, one of the platoon members,
goes over to inspect the dead. As one of the Japanese soldiers
springs to his feet, bayonet in hand, Red's gun jams. He turns
and runs, screeching for help. Croft captures the Japanese soldier
But as the new prisoner leans against a tree and lights a cigarette,
Croft nonchalantly raises his gun and shoots him. In the second
example, Roth, another platoon member, finds a little bird with a
broken wing. Croft, correct in assuming that there is no room in

the new power structure for sentiment, fails nevertheless to control
his personal emotion. He crushes the bird to death in his bare hands
and tosses the lifeless carcass aside as the men watch, horrified.
As Mailer has painstakingly argued through General Cummings, emotions
must be controlled absolutely if personal power is ever to be transferred into manipulation of others on a sustained level.

Such absolute viciousness as Croft displays engenders absolute
fear on the part of the members of Croft's patrol. It allows Croft
to maintain control of his miniature version of Cummings' power
structure so long as that fear is not transferred and so long as the
hatred of the men for Croft is transferred to a designated enemy.
An example of this transferrance occurs when the men climb the
mountain and Croft pushes them on, almost past the point of total
fatigue; they try to make him turn back but his awesome courage prevents them from doing so. On this simple level, the Cummings plan
works; "they had discovered that they could not hate him and do anything about it, so they hated the mountain, hated it with more ferver
than they could ever have hated a human being." They continue to
climb. According to Mailer, the only thing that can, and finally does,
defeat Croft and the men like him, is the chance occurance that
allows the men either to break free of the fear they have had, or
to stop the continuity of transference of hatred upon the target
designated by the manipulator. While it is true the manipulator
can only be defeated by chance, the odds are that the chance happening
necessary will always occur, since the system admits of no flex-
ibility at all.

Although only fortune can defeat Croft and Cummings, many men, unaware of this maxim, which their creator has imposed upon them, still try. These men illustrate Mailer's view of what happens to the individual under such a system. The first of these men is General Cummings' aide, Lieutenant Hearn. He becomes Croft's commanding officer on the reconnaissance mission to Mt. Anaka. Hearn takes command of the mission because General Cummings has sent him. Cummings wants Hearn out of the way. Croft has him killed by having Hearn walk into an ambush.

As a social type, Hearn represents the rich, intellectual, sons of the upper class who see their parents as having gained economic power at the expense of the lower classes, and yet are not quite ready to give up that inherited power. Mailer speculated about the reasons behind Hearn's inability to successfully wrest power from those who have it in a "Time Machine" episode called "The Addled Womb." Mailer paints Hearn's upper-middle class Midwestern background of country club, prep school, and Harvard. Hearn's room-mate at Harvard tries to get into a "correct" club, and his efforts to do so awaken Hearn's latent scorn for the established order. Hearn switches majors to English after a few discussions awaken him to the intellectual world of Mann and Marlowe. He joins the John Reed Society and becomes an avowed Marxist. Of course, he rejects his family's wealth. Finally the president of the John Reed Society asks him to quit. He tells Hearn:

> "If a man moves to the party because of spiritual
> or intellectual reasons, he's bound to move away

again once the particular psychological climate that
moved him there in the first place is changed. It's
the man who comes to the party because economic in-
equities humiliate him every day of his life who
makes a good Communist." [p343]

So Hearn finds himself in limbo in the power system. He has rejected the upper-middle class availability of power and has in turn
been rejected by those dedicated to overthrowing that power.

Before the war, Hearn had tried a few different ways to change
the system rather than change himself; he became first a labor organizer. When this occupation soured on him he returned to his
father's society. At parties he noticed that although socially
powerful, his father's friends had achieved that power by relinquishing
their own individuality and potency:

There is a migratory party almost every night from house
to house along Lake Shore Drive, and the wives and hus-
bands are always mixed, always drunk. It is all done in
a random, rather irritable kind of lust, and the petting
is more frequent than the cuckolding. [pp. 350-51]

When he becomes an Army officer, he discovers that the officers
he comes in contact with are quite the same as his father's friends.
He holds them in contempt, seeing them as rather shallow men interested
in nothing more than food and physical comfort. As a matter of fact,
he feels superior to everyone, especially the enlisted men. But he
cannot bring himself to admit it, and so vacillates between guilt
over his power and position and envy for those with more power and

position. Thus, of the troops he thinks, in the typical manner of
an upper-class liberal who feels guilt:

> They slept with mud and insects and worms while the
>
> officers bitched because there were no paper napkins
>
> and the chow could stand improvement. [p.76]

And yet he admires General Cummings' ability to "extend his thoughts
into immediate and effective action." At the same time, he is aware
of Cummings' "trace of effeminancy."

Hearn's physical description of the general implies he is aware
that the Army power structure is identical to the power structure of
other modes of life as well. Hearn says of Cummings, "his expression
when he smiled was very close to the ruddy complacent and hard appearance of any number of American senators and businessmen." Once
Cummings reveals to Hearn his contempt of the power structure and
his dreams for the future, Hearn tells Cummings that if his policies
are followed and America loses the war, revolution will follow. But
the general tells him "You're misreading history if you see this war
as a grand revolution. It's power concentration." What this concentration means to the common man, says Cummings, is that his natural
state is anxiety. To prove the soundness of his ideas on power,
Cummings invites Hearn to a game of chess—each man playing by his
own philosophy. Cummings dominates the game entirely.

Cummings knows the major reason why Hearn is such a minimal
opposition is that he is still unsure whether he opposes Cummings
or is just like him. In order to win Hearn over to his side completely, Cummings orders him to supervise the setting up of the

officer's recreation tent. As he carries out that order, Hearn discovers "with a shock . . . the trace of contempt he was beginning to feel for an enlisted man." He realizes the truth of the general's lesson that in functioning as an officer he must assume the emotional prejudices of that class. He begins to realize that the real reason he is contemptuous of his fellow officers is that he is afraid he is in reality exactly like them. Yet, as he begins to find his place and to achieve a kind of autonomy, he does become a threat to Cummings' sense of absolute control, a possible rival. So Cummings decides to test Hearn's strength. He sends him out on the almost impossible mission of buying supplies from a passing liberty ship. Hearn tackles the assignment successfully, using his liberal, rather than Cummings' fascist, techniques. He reasons rather than applies psychological pressure, he bribes rather than coerces. Armed with this success he proceeds back to Cummings' tent. But Cummings is not there. So, in more than a symbolic protest Hearn stamps a cigarette out in the middle of the fastidious general's spotless floor. When Cummings gets back to his tent and looks around, he sees this emblem of his defeat.

> A deep pang of pain and fear lanced through his chest.
> On the middle of his floor was the match and the cig-
> arette butt, mashed into the duckboards in a tangled
> ugly excrement of black ash, soiled paper, and brown
> tobacco. [p. 317]

For Mailer, excrement is a recurring symbol of defeat. Earlier in
The Naked and the Dead, in narrating the death of Hennessy during

the landing on the island, Mailer tells how the boy had defecated shortly before he ran out of his foxhole screaming. Hennessy knew he was defeated because all of the veterans of the other battles had told him that everything would be all right so long as he "kept a tight asshole." Mailer uses this symbol in An American Dream and Why Are We In Vietnam as well. Based on the soldier's idea of "kissing ass," too, is Mailer's idea that the rectum symbolizes subservience and sterile self gratification. To contemplate one's own excrement is for Mailer the epitome of egoism without ego expansion. Perhaps this idea explains why Mailer wrote in Cannibals and Christians that "ambitious societies loathe scatological themes and are obsessed with them."

After seeing the crushed cigarette, Cummings looks about the room and sees a note from Hearn. What follows is the third and last confrontation between the two men before Cummings sends Hearn on the mission to the mountain from which he does not expect Hearn to return. The climax of that confrontation comes when Cummings orders Hearn to pick up the cigarette. The general has won the battle. Even though he will eventually lose the war, at this stage the general and his kind seem invincible.

Thus, in the incipient stages of the new power morality system, the common soldier seems more or less powerless against the awesome strength of the American fascist, as Mailer projects him. And not only is there no effective opposition from the common soldier, there does not seem to be any effectively organized liberal opposition from the upper class, if Hearn is an example of it. Near the end he is more

power rival than power opposition, a fact demonstrated by his thoughts
while leading the I and R platoon:

> Beyond Cummings, deeper now, was his own desire to lead
> the platoon. It had grown, ignited suddenly, become one
> of the most satisfying things he had ever done. He could
> understand Croft's staring at the mountain through the
> field glasses or killing the bird. When he searched him-
> self, he was just another Croft. [p.580]

Something that Cummings once said to him comes to mind; it brings
his real desires into focus.

> Cummings had once said, "You know, Robert, there really
> are only two kinds of liberals and radicals. There are
> the ones who are afraid of the world and want it changed
> to benefit themselves, the Jew liberalism sort of thing.
> And then there are the young people who don't understand
> their desires. They want to remake the world, but they
> never admit they want it in their own image." [p.580]

Hearn realizes that he is of the second type. He is still afraid of
Cummings and contemptuous of the men below him. In short, he finally
fits into the Cummings fear ladder and desires to strengthen his position by continuing to lead the patrol. He knows that if he forfeits
his leadership to Croft and goes back he will again be outside of
the power structure, hence impotent.

Hearn is aware that somehow he must oppose Cummings and his
power structure, but does not know how. He toys with the idea of
resigning his commission when he returns from the patrol around

Mt. Anaku, but he believes too much in the power system and the
fear ladder to think of doing such a thing seriously. Besides,
he is beginning to enjoy his new found power, and he knows he will
need all the personal power he can muster for the struggle for social
autonomy he envisions will occur after the war is over.

> If the world turned Fascist, if Cummings had his cen-
> tury, there was a little thing he could do. There was
> always terrorism. But a neat terrorism with nothing
> sloppy about it, no machine guns, no grenades, no bombs,
> nothing messy, no indiscriminate killing. Merely the
> knife and the garrote, a few trained men, and a list of
> fifty bastards to be knocked off, then another fifty. [p.585]

The conclusion that Mailer seems to be drawing is that the loss of
power of the individual in America is inherent in the type of society
it is, and has no regard for social position or class. As the "Time
Machine" on General Cummings reinforces, even he is a bit of the
argil and not the mold, that the mold is society. The only hope left
is that a man can be an individual and stand against the grain of
society. The rest of the novel is an exploration of the various ways
of becoming an individual. Mailer explores the possibility of personal autonomy within the prescribed power system by using the various members of Croft's I and R platoon as guinea pigs. As Cummings
points out, the natural state for the common man is anxiety. Throughout the novel Mailer portrays many manifestations of this foreboding.

Chief among the anxieties of the men is their worry over what
is happening at home. For example, Mailer gives very vividly in

part II, chapter 5 a description of a guard duty where each man
when alone first dreams of his wife at home. But these dreams soon
become more and more erotic, culminating in the frustration of mas-
terbation coupled with scenes of marital infidelity the men imagine
taking place at home. This is the first time Mailer equates the
loss of individual power with onanism. It is an equation which
will play an increasingly important role in Mailer's fiction. The
men of the platoon sing about their anxiety over what is happening
at home a bit more drolly in the scene Mailer calls "Chorus: Women."

The men exhibit great anxiety, also, over even so basic a
question as who or what they are. In chapter II of part 7, for
example, some of the men of the I and R platoon get very drunk and
go off to seek Japanese corpses in order to loot the bodies for
souvenirs. The dead are in various states of dismemberment and
decay. The sight makes profound but varied impressions on each of
the men. Red Valsen muses on the idea that they were once men, with
separate childhoods and dreams of the future. Being a man of the
soil, "he realized that in a little while the fetidness of this corpse
would seep into the earth and be lost, but now it was horrible in
its stench." Finally Red decides that "there damn sure ain't anything
special about a man if he can smell as bad as he does when he's dead."
At that point, if Cummings is right, Red is at the bottom of the fear
ladder. As long as he stays there he will be a fit soldier. Then,
in grotesque parody of Dachau, Martinez smashes in the skull of one
of the corpses and steals its gold teeth. But as he does so, he is
aware that like the dead corpses he too means nothing.

And yet, the struggle to find meaning, the struggle against the forces which Cummings outlines and Croft practices, goes on. In addition to Hearn's futile opposition against the forces, Red Valsen, Woodrow Wilson, Goldstein, Ridges, Wyman, Brown, Stanley, Gallager, Roth, Polack, Martinez, and Minetta also struggle in their own ways.

Red Valsen has been struggling all his life. As the "Time Machine" episode concerning him makes clear, his Army existence parallels his civilian life. Red is a skeptic; he does not fall for the obviously emotion laden speeches of a Communist labor organizer while he is still a civilian. He understands that the organizer is really trying to gain control over him through the union. In the Army, Red easily figures out that his commanding officers are really after personal power, even more than they are out to win the war. And yet, he does not know how to fight the manipulators. Because he doesn't, he is manipulated in turn.

Woodrow Wilson plays a twofold role. Not only is he an individual soldier who fails to achieve any personal power, he is also a symbolic representation of the failure of the idealism of the president Woodrow Wilson. The title of his "Time Machine," "The Invincible," is as bitterly ironic as the slogan "the war to end all wars;" it makes the parallels between the defeated president and the defeated soldier that much closer. Just as the collapse of President Wilson's peace plans brought on a new power struggle among the world's, as well as America's, political and military leaders, the collapse of the soldier Woodrow Wilson brings on the symbolic power struggle between Croft, the "fascist," and Hearn, the liberal. The journey

to take Wilson back to the beach after he is wounded is symbolic.
His four litter bearers begin in a spirit of comradeship, but as
they go further, they become so weary of the burden of carrying
Wilson that they are soon attacking one another on very personal
grounds. Finally, Brown and Stanley give up, admit they are defeated, and drop out. Ridges and Goldstein, however, refuse to
give up. "Wilson was a burden they could not leave." Ridges comes
to think of his task almost literally as a cross to bear. In fact,
throughout much of the journey, he tries to convert Wilson. Symbolically his efforts become an attempt to convert President Wilson's
secular ideal of peace into an act of Christian suffering. But
Ridges is not successful.

Even after Wilson dies, Ridges and Goldstein continue to carry
him, refusing to believe he is dead and that what they have been
working so hard to accomplish was for nothing. When they finally
do lose the body to the swift moving currents of a mountain stream,
Ridges, for the first time, rails out at God. Goldstein, however,
recalls the words of his old grandfather about the necessity for
enduring through suffering. "There was nothing in him at the moment,
nothing but a vague anger, a deep resentment, and the origins of a
vast hopelessness." It is this hopelessness that gives birth to
Mailer's existential philosophy. He nurtures it in Barbary Shore.
It grows to maturity in An American Dream. It is this hopelessness
that eats its own child in Why Are We In Vietnam? And yet Mailer
still portrays some hope for the individual in this chapter about the
struggle to carry Wilson, because it ends with the symbolic act of

Goldstein sharing his canteen with Ridges.

In another "Time Machine" episode Mailer traces Joey Goldstein's
philosophy of life to his grandfather. The grandfather equates
suffering with the will to endure. Joey himself dreams of enduring
by someday opening his own welding shop--a humble form of individualism. His is an idealized portrait of a man who has been able to
balance individualism with social responsibility. But he can only
do so for a while. In a conversation between Martinez and Goldstein,
Mailer reveals the weakness that renders Goldstein incapable of at-
taining power in the sort of world system Cummings portrays.

> Goldstein was too affectionate to possess any real de-
> fenses; at the first positive hint of friendship he was
> ready to forget all his grievances and respond with
> warmth and simplicity. [p.448]

Too much compassion is precisely the charge that Hitler used against
the Jews in his pleas to the German people for the Master Race.
Goldstein reveals his absolute naivete when he says, "I really
believe in being honest and sincere in business; all the really
big men got where they are through decency." So here is another
man destined to become subordinate in the power structure. And yet
although he will never amass power he does have a chance to achieve
autonomy. The only other man to succeed in achieveing a degree of
autonomy in the novel, Ridges, is sustained by his simple but naive
religious attitude.

The other soldiers never achieve either autonomy or power: Wyman
unsuccessfully attempts through scapegoating to achieve at least a

semblance of power. But what he achieves is, at best, self delusion.
Sergeant Brown, one of the two men who fails to carry Woodrow Wilson
back (who fails symbolically, that is, to achieve power or autonomy),
is portrayed ironically enough as the typical American boy. Brown's
story is a Willy Loman tale of middle class complacency. His Army
rank of Sergeant coincides with his civilian rank of salesman; he
is higher on the power scale than men like Stanley or Gallagher,
but not much. Corporal Stanley attempts to gain personal power
by attaching himself to people who can help him advance; but this
does not get him very far. Gallagher, on the other hand, had tried
in civilian life to gain personal power by joining Right Wing groups
in Boston. In relating his life story, Mailer portrays another side
of the power-fear ladder. Men near the bottom, such as Gallagher,
know they are being victimized but they really do not know by whom.
And so they are impotent to do anything. And ironically, their
attempts to gain autonomy and personal power result in a further
weakening of both. The mere immensity of the Cummings power system
victimizes individuals simply by overwhelming their individuality.
Cummings sees the individuals merely as troops to be manipulated
statistically. Gallagher sees the power structure above him as something huge, overwhelming, and amorphous: International Jews, perhaps,
or Communists, or Fascists, or all three, he does not know. But
whatever it is, it causes anxiety in him. When he learns that his
wife died in giving birth to his child, his only consolation, like
Babbitt's, is that perhaps his son will do better in life than he has.

Roth, the agnostic Jew, tries to think of himself not as a Jew but

as an American. Assimilation into a new culture, however, is never
an intellectual process only. Almost always it involves time,
usually two or three generations at least. Roth may think of himself as just a white Anglo-Saxon American, but he is not. The
other members of the platoon constantly remind him of this fact.
Their rejection and antagonism of Roth give them a scapegoat, someone even lower on the fear-ladder than they are. Thus, picking
on Roth gives them a chance to exert some autonomy and power of
their own.

While Cummings and Croft have been able to amass personal power
because they have learned to trust their paranoia, Polack has not.
He remains indecisive because he does not know who to trust. In
the power structure emerging out of the war, a structure based upon
a very mobile social caste system, the ability to make decisions
alone and very quickly and to manipulate others is absolutely essential to one's amassing personal power and autonomy.

In order to show how men at the top can manipulate the men at
the bottom, Mailer uses Martinez to demonstrate that men like him
can be conditioned the same way Pavlov conditioned dogs. Mailer
shows Minetta, on the other hand, in a conscious attempt to overcome this conditioning through the use of role playing. Minetta
tries to get out of the Army on a section 8. The medics know that
he is faking but cannot prove it. It is his own inability to continue
faking that defeats him and sends him back to the war. The ability
to play roles is essential for survival in the emerging social system
as Mailer sees it, a system based heavily upon what will come to

be called charisma during the era of John Kennedy's presidency.

For the officers, the problem is to achieve autonomy through power; many of the enlisted men try to achieve power through autonomy. Neither task is possible because, though they may seem to be, power and autonomy are not related. In addition, both are controlled by chance. It is the inability of both Cummings and Croft to compensate for chance, it will be recalled, that defeats them. At this stage of his developement it is Mailer's hope that in the real post World War II world the Cummings' fascist system will be defeated for the same reason.

Because of chance happenings Cummings is finally overwhelmed by his own beauracracy. It robs him of victory and of final control. To see how bureaucracy overwhelmes the troops and robs them of their dignity and sense of perspective, one need look no further than the scenes depicting mail call. For example, in chapter III, 9, the mail comes in while the men are working to build the road to the front lines. Gallagher is waiting to hear from his wife. Her baby is due. As the men read their letters, or have them read to them, they are mentally transported back to civilian life. And the image each of the men evokes shows how closely their civilian and Army lives parallel. When mail comes for Hennessey, one of the mail clerks remembers he was "knocked off" and stamps the letters addressed to the dead soldier "Addressee Killed in Action."

> The return address on the letters was "Mom and Dad,
>
> 12 Riverdale Avenue, Tacuhet, Indiana." The assistant
>
> read it to himself, and thought for a moment of a

thousand billboard ads for soft drinks and mouthwashes

and toothpastes. "Gee, isn't that sad," he said.

"Yeah, it sure is."

"Makes you think," the assistant said. [p.262]

Then Gallagher is told by the chaplain that his wife died in child-
birth. After a few days the letters from his wife start coming in
because of the mail delays. He cannot accept the fact of her death.
He tries to think of her as being in the same time sequence as the
letters. Finally he gets the last one and has a mental breakdown
rather than open it and face the truth.

To see how bureaucracy overwhelms men like Cummings, men with
dreams of absolute power, all one need do is trace the final days
of the Anopopei campaign. In chapter III, 13, Cummings is preparing
for the final assault on the Toyaku line. He is fascinated with
the idea of attacking Toyaku from the rear. But this would entail
Naval support. He goes over to G-3 (the division in charge of
operations and training). The officer in charge is Major Dalleson,
the perfect beauraucrat. He is dedicated to performing his function.
"It was inconceivable to Major Dalleson that he should desert the
General unless he were ordered to; he would, if the bivouac had been
overrun by Japanese troops, probably have died defending the General
in his tent." In other words, he personally is no threat to the
Cummings power ladder, but the bureaucracy he represents is. This
bit of information Cummings does not discover until it is too late.
When he goes off to try to beg Naval support he leaves Dalleson in
charge. Dalleson is in trouble because he has allowed Cummings'

troops to advance too far. The troops are penetrating closer and
closer to the Toyaku Line. The corpses they are finding along the
way seem to be much too skinny, and Dalleson cannot figure out why.
As the troops advance more it dawns on him that he has inadvertently
mounted a full attack--two thirds of the Japanese supplies have been
captured and General Toyaku and one half of his staff have been
killed. By the next morning, Dalleson learns, there are 1500 American
troops behind the Japanese line, and by the afternoon the flanks
have been rolled up. Cummings returns, having been granted a destroyer. He cannot call the destroyer back without appearing to his
rivals for power to have made a mistake, so he allows the destroyer
to shell the Toyaku Line even though it is a totally useless gesture.
Cummings has been "defeated;" he has misjudged his opponent's strength
and now chance has given his victory to Major Dalleson, who doesn't
even realize what he has done. Nobody really controlled the war because
nobody controls a bureaucracy. So America, Mailer seemed to be saying,
despite all the efforts of men to control and aim its destiny, was
adrift politically and in danger of crashing on some Barbary shore.
In his next novel, Mailer attempted to trace the reason for the
aimless drift, and the direction the tides and winds of circumstance
were taking.

Chapter II Notes

[1]
Norman Mailer, Advertisements For Myself, (New York, G.P. Putnam's Sons, 1959), p. 24.

[2] Norman Mailer, The Naked and the Dead (New York, Rinehart and Company, 1948), p. 82. [all subsequent citations are to this edition and are given in brackets].

Chapter III   Barbary Shore

Barbary Shore was written during the height of the beatnik,
or hipster, movement, and the vogue in certain American intellectual
circles for existentialism. The unofficial headquarters in the
United States for both of these fads was the section of New York
City known as Greenwich Village, or simply, The Village. In the
years shortly before and after writing Barbary Shore, Norman Mailer
was very much a part of what was called the "village scene." Although
he did spend some time away from New York, most notably at the
Sorbonne, much of the three years between The Naked and the Dead
and Barbary Shore were spent cofounding and writing for a small
newspaper called The Village Voice.

The Village Voice was a mirror of the times. Many of the writers
in fashion during the beatnik years were discussed, reviewed, and
published on the pages of the Voice. From these authors Mailer
gleaned a number of ideas, and much argot and slang. Such words
as "hip," "orgiastic," "anal," "onanism," and others appeared frequently
in Mailer's nonfiction during this period. In these years Mailer
was greatly influenced by the psychologists Robert Linder and Wilhelm
Reich. The ideas Mailer learned from these writers found their way
into Barbary Shore and Mailer's subsequent fiction.

Because of these new influences, and because Mailer did not want
to rest his career on the laurels of The Naked and the Dead (by writing,
as he called it, The Naked and the Dead Go to Japan), his second
novel was very different from its predecessor. Barbary Shore is,

indeed, a major shift in Mailer's fictional technique and philosophical intent. He labels the book the "first existentialist novel in America," and takes up the same task that he assigns to his hero and narrator, Mickey Lovett. Mailer abandons both the techinques and the sympathy for the masses that he had learned from such writers as Steinbeck and the early John Dos Passos. In Barbary Shore Mailer began to concern himself only with the strivings of those people who have the potential for autonomy, for "existential freedom," or "hip," as he termed it, in what he viewed as an overwhelmingly oppressive and barbaric society. In Barbary Shore the realistic descriptions of the forces and actions are likewise gone. In this, his second novel, Mailer was more preoccupied with speculations about the effects of power on autonomy.

Arriving at the conclusion that the failure of the Marxist revolution in Russia also meant that all hope of overturning the emerging bureaucracy of monopoly capitalism in America was lost, Mailer turned his attention to a search for a protagonist who could achieve personal freedom in spite of the newly emerging social system which proposed nothing more than a surrealistic existence. Too, Mailer wanted a protagonist with whom he could explore the role of the serious artist in such a surrealistic, aimless world.

So Mailer created Mikey Lovett to be the hero and first-person narrator of Barbary Shore. Symbolically and literally, Lovett has no past. Because of some accident during the war, he has lost both his memory and his face. Like Sergius O'Shaugnessy after him, Lovett has mere mental form without shape. He must shape his own existence and give it meaning.

As might be expected in a first-person narrative, some of
the protagonist's conditions were the author's own. Mailer and
Lovett have much in common. For example, in Advertisements for
Myself, Mailer described the success of The Naked and the Dead
as being a lobotomy to his past. It will be recalled that the
same operation was performed on Mikey Lovett as a result of the
war which his psyche so violently rejected. Lovett also refused
to be overwhelmed by the wearying banality of conformist society.
Mailer threw his lot in with the non-conformist "hipsters." Lovett
rejected the present political and social system. Mailer backed
the socialist canididate for president, Henry Wallace.

Lovett affirmed his refusal to be overwhelmed by banality at
the beginning of his narrative in the scenes in which a commercially
successful playwright, Willie Dinsmore (Will he din us more), gave
Lovett some Polonius-like platitudes and his "writer's retreat," a
run-down room in a run-down boarding house which Dinsmore had vacated
in order to spend some time in the country. Of Dinsmore, Lovett
says, "like so many writers he had very little interest in people,
and if they could serve his didactic needs, a pigeonhole was all
he required." When Dinsmore says, "there are the haves and the
have-nots . . . there are the progressive countries and the reactionary
countries. In half the globe the people own the means of production,
and in the other half the fascists have control," Lovett rejects the
older writer's platitudes as grotesques, reminiscent of those which
fill the old writer's notebook in Sherwood Anderson's Winesburg,

Ohio, a novel with which both Mailer and Lovett are quite familiar. In *Advertisements for Myself*, Mailer has an essay on David Riesman. In that essay is a quotation from Anderson's "The Book of the Grotesque" which illustrates some of the old writer's platitudes and says,

> Every man and every institution sees itself through its own eyes, and there are probably few situations on earth whose moral judgments cannot be reversed to provide the illusion of equal truth. Intellectual penetration of this sort can never fail, but on the other hand it can never succeed for it is merely a flipping of the switches, a change of polarities, and the platitude turned on its head is still a platitude.[1]

Lovett reveals his vague knowledge of *Winesburg, Ohio* when his girl friend, Lannie, attempts to pass off one of the grotesques--the story of Wing Biddlebaum--as real. Lovett tells her, "Why I read that . . . it's a story." Lovett knows that an ideology must be lived and paid for through suffering, not thinking. Thus, Dinsmore's advice to Lovett is worthless.

But even if he is of no real worth to Lovett, Dinsmore is of some economic and physical comfort. The playwright is successful in talking his landlady, Guinevere, into allowing Mikey Lovett to rent the old writing room. Unlike the playwright, who used the room only as a quiet retreat from his family, Mikey Lovett moves in and lives there. The boarding house is a perfect setting for Mailer to portray what he called the "air of our time, authority and nihilism

stalking each other in the orgiastic hollow of this century." Mailer
equated authority and nihilism in Barbary Shore with "'State capitalism' and 'monopoly capitalism,' and how each is kept in working order
by comparable groups of increasingly totalitarian bureaucrats."

The world of Barbary Shore is one in which appearance and reality
are confused. The name of the landlady, Guinevere, is a clue to
Mailer's interpretation of this problem of confusion. Like Malory's
Le Morte d'Arthur, Mailer's novel is concerned with building an
ordered world out of barbarous anarchy. Both Malory's and Mailer's
societies are in danger of failing because their principals can never
really see each other for what they are. Thus, in Malory's tale
Balin and Balan slay each other and so seal the kingdom's ultimate
fate because each cannot recognize his own brother beneath the armor
of war. Hollingsworth slays McLeod because he cannot understand who
McLeod really is. Arthur's queen is unfaithful because she rejects
his merely intellectual devotion. McLeod loses Guinevere to Hollingsworth
for the same reason. Men in Malory are wounded or slain because they
falsely wear the armour of other men. It is Lovett's task to try to
order the chaotic world of Barbary Shore before the same thing occurs
to him and his world. The quests that Lovett must accomplish before
he can begin to order his world include finding his own key to life
and identifying the masks that people wear and the roles they play.
Mailer shows Lovett doing all of these things throughout the novel.

His first task, and he accomplishes it slowly, is to find out
who the people he lives with really are behind the masks of social
convention that they wear. For example, it seems at first that

McLeod and Hollingsworth are simply other boarders. But gradually

Lovett learns that McLeod is really Guinevere's husband, the father

of Monina, a former revolutionary, a former American bureaucrat,

and perhaps even a former FBI informer. At first Hollingsworth

seems to be working for a stock brokerage firm, but then it turns

out he is really an agent for a government agency, presumably the

FBI, and finally it seems that he is working for himself in order

to get the "little object" that McLeod has. Much of what there is

of plot concerns this attempt by Hollingsworth to get that "little

object" from McLeod. What that "little object" is has been a constant

question among critics since the novel's introduction in 1951. An

answer is forthcoming, but must be postponed for now until after the

major characters have been analyzed. It is upon their personalities

and what those personalities symbolize that the answer is based.

The first person who must be taken into consideration is the

narrator, Mikey Lovett. As stated above, because of his amnesia

Lovett has no past. This fact is further complicated because even

his face is not his own; it is a plastic surgeon's conception of a

face. Lovett does not even know how old he is. Sometimes, when

some details of his past do flow in his mind, he does not even know

if they are real or something he might have read. He lives only for

the present. He views life in the way someone watching a commercial

on television does; often he is not able to distinguish what is real

from what is an extrapolation of reality. This problem is evident

in his description of Guinevere. "It was difficult," he says, "to

forget her breasts which had thrust upward from their binding in

copious splendor, so palpable that they obtained the intensification of
art and became more real than themselves." Lovett has pretensions to
art himself; he wants to become a novelist.

> I intended a large ambitious work about an immense in-
> stitution never defined more exactly than that and about
> the people who wandered through it. The book had a hero
> and a heroine, but they never met while they were in the
> institution. It was only when they escaped, each of them
> in separate ways and by separate methods, that they were
> capable of love and so could discover each other.[2]

He could be describing his own plight--or that of the men of
The Naked and the Dead. The plight is precisely that it is often
impossible to escape the institution. To argue this point Mailer
shows how Lovett himself is caught up in the little society of the
boarding house. Lovett says, "If I lived in a close relationship
with the few people I knew in the rooming house and became progres-
sively less capable of doing without them, there is after all a
precedent." Among the people upon whom he becomes dependent are
McLeod, the fastidious gentleman who lives on one side of him, and
Hollingsworth, the messy gentleman on the other side. He becomes
very friendly with McLeod and often spends hours talking to him.
At the same time he is becoming more fascinated with Guinevere, his
landlady. From the descriptions of her appearance and actions it
becomes apparent that she symbolizes the hedonism and narcissism
of post World War II society. As the conversations between Lovett
and McLeod continue through the novel it becomes apparent that McLeod

is really a personification of the Marxist movement in America.
Hollingsworth tries to get friendly with Lovett, and partially
achieves his aim. They sometimes talk, but Lovett always feels
as if he were talking to a machine. Hollingsworth is, in fact,
a personification of the faceless American bureaucracy. That he
is often in the novel described as a faceless machine is appropriate.
As Mailer reaffirmed in Cannibals and Christians,

> The essence of totalitarianism is that it beheads. It
> beheads individuality, variety, dissent, extreme pos-
> sibility, romantic faith; it blinds vision, deadens
> instinct; it obliterates the past. It makes factories
> look like college campuses or mental hospitals where once
> factories had the specific beauty of revealing their
> huge and sometimes brutal function. . . . The totalitarian
> impulse not only washes away distinctions but looks for
> a style in buildings, in clothing, and in the ornamentaions
> of tools, appliances, and daily objects which will diminish
> one's sense of reality by reducing such emotions as awe,
> dread, beauty, pity, terror, calm, horror, and harmony.
> By dislocating us from the most powerful emotions of reality,
> totalitarianism leaves us further isolated in the empty
> landscapes of psychosis, precisely that inner landscape
> of void and dread which we flee by turning to totalitarian
> styles of life.[3]

Hollingsworth is, in fact, a type of cannibal, as Mailer defined the
type in Cannibals and Christians:

[Cannibals include] all of that persecuted Right Wing

which sees itself as martyr, knows that it knows how

to save the world: one can save the world by killing

off what is second-rate. So they are Cannibals--they

believe that survival and health of the species comes

from consuming one's own, not one's near-own, but one's

own species . . . to kill and to eliminate is his

sense of human continuation.[4]

Lovett learns that Hollingsworth is a government agent sent to

interrogate McLeod, a former Marxist labor leader. In keeping with

his allegorical role, McLeod reveals that he has studied Marxist doc-

trine, led strikes, and become an important member of the American

Central Committee, traveling frequently to Moscow. But after Stalin

gained control of the Soviet Union, McLeod dropped out of the party

completely, thinking of himself as a failure. He is a failure, but

not for the reasons he suspects. Mostly he has failed because he has

spent his life intellectualizing rather than living. Mailer points to

this failure as a major psychic root of America's social problems.

What makes it worse is that McLeod's intellectualizations are often

no more than grotesques, as far from compassion as they are from reality.

He says, for example,

A campaign of vigorous terrorism must be undertaken to

wrest the seats of power from the buh-geoisie. The

president must be assassinated, and congressmen imprisoned.

The State Department and Wall Street must be liquidated,

libraries must be burned, and the filthy polluted South

must be destroyed nigh unto the last stone with the ex-

ception of the Negroes. [p.58]

McLeod must view his struggle in terms of war, because, as Mailer

wrote in Cannibals and Christians,

The health of Communism, its secret neccessity, is

an enemy external to itself; war is indeed the health

of the totalitarian state, and peace is its disease.

Communism would split and rupture and war upon itself

if ever it occupied most of the world, for then it

would have to solve the problems of most of the world

and those problems are not soluble in the rigidity of

a system.[5]

Meanwhile, a new tenant, Lannie Madison, has rented a room in

the boarding house. As her name (MADison) and her actions (such as

placing the couch so that it faces the wall, and painting her room,

even the windows, black) suggest, she represents the kind of confused

hopelessness that many of the idealists of the period felt after the

death of Trotsky, the idol of her youth. Because she holds McLeod

partly responsible for the assassination of Trotsky, Hollingsworth

is able to bribe Lannie Madison with a case of whisky to assist him

in breaking down McLeod. She does. Her conception of idealism is

so degenerated, so perverse, by this time that her most compassionate

act in the novel is giving a bum in the park a bottle, in parody, per-

haps, of Marx's notion that religion is the opiate of the people. Often

she confuses reality and fiction, as in the scene mentioned above in

which she regards the story of Wing Biddlebaum not as a symbol of her own history or a parable for her own actions, but as a part of her own true history. Sometimes she goes even further. For example, she tells Lovett that a mouse in her room is Christ, and after a while she accepts her own symbol literally. It is in this acceptance of her own symbolism that she represents the "Lane of Madison," or Madison Avenue, the original street of dreams. And it is in this capacity that she finally wears down McLeod's revolutionary spirit.

But when McLeod is alone with Lovett the ex-revolutionary begins to indoctrinate the writer. As the novel progresses Lovett comes more and more to accept McLeod's enthusiasm while remaining undecided about his doctrine. What keeps him most skeptical is the fact that McLeod's marriage to Guinevere is such a failure, and that the offspring of that marriage—of the revolutionary spirit and the masses—is Monina, a personification of the narcisstic post war generation. Her mother is quick to assure Lovett that Monina's future lies in Hollywood. Mailer traces such a future in The Deer Park. The marriage has failed precisely because McLeod has never been able to accept any but intellectual union. For him love is nothing more than a crutch that helps one, as he says, "rear back and look at the cosmos." As the interrogation becomes more intense, it becomes more apparent that Hollingsworth has been sent to get the "little object" which McLeod apparently stole from a government bureau he once worked for. Hollingsworth does not know what the "little object" is but assumes it to be of material worth and so wants it for himself.

Meanwhile, under McLeod's guidance, Lovett has made for himself a vision of the dehumanization of monopoly capitalism. McLeod's doctrine teaches that as production becomes more mechanized and machines more costly, more people will be enslaved economically as businesses expand in an effort to show a profit. But McLeod also sees a similar danger in state capitalism, in which "the worker would be paid less and obliged to pay more." Such a situation would mean the gradual regimentation and enslavement of labor and "the saturation of the working-class mind to propaganda until even the mating bed became a duty." Thus, under either monopoly or state capitalism the troops would remain troops. Mailer restated this idea many years later when he wrote in Cannibals and Christians

> In a civilization whose compassion is of political use
> and is stratified in welfare programs which do not build
> a better society but shore up a worse; in a world whose
> ultimate logic is war, because in a world of war all
> overproduction is possible since peoples and communities
> may be destroyed wholesale—in a breath . . . .[6]

Ultimately McLeod sees the human function of socialism "is to raise mankind to a higher level of suffering, for given the hypothesis that man has certain tragic contradictions, the alternative is between a hungry belly and a hungry mind, but fulfillment there is never." It is at this point that Lovett begins to wonder about the validity of McLeod's confusing social responsibility (the hungry belly) with the responsibility of the individual (the hungry mind). It is also at this time that Lovett learns of the homosexual affair between Lannie and Guinevere—between despair and the masses, between the masses and the media of Madison Avenue—which Guinevere soon grows tired of. Learning that Guinevere outgrows Lannie quickly gives Lovett hope for the future.

In the closing scenes of the book, McLeod comes to the full realization that "the revolution has failed to come," and that "our problem is not to end the exploitation but to resolve contradictions in the economic structure. Indeed, we may have been wrong all the time, and the bourgeoisie have been right. Man is only capable of founding societies based on privilege and inequality." But McLeod removes himself from the social ramifications of his failure by going back to economics. He reverts, that is, to theory again, explaining that capitalism must be imperialistic since it is based upon continual growth which leads ultimately to war or collapse of society. He cites the failure of the revolution of 1918 to improve the plight of the troops in lieu of the increased industrialization, or "state capitalism," a colossus which must stride the same path as monopoly capitalism because it, too, cannot improve productivity and hence must depend upon "seizing new countries, stripping them of their wealth, and converting their economy to war. In short, plunder." What this corollary points to is the failure of free enterprise and its ultimate destruction because all the discontent it causes among workers will lead to random sabotage which will eventually be controlled by a growing police force, and hence a growth in the police state. This growth of totalitarianism would result in "state profit and state surveillance, state-enforced poverty and state-endowed wealth. The bureaucrat drives his limousine and he is the only one. Poor proletariat. Cheated still another time. They are fed the turnips

their masters would have them become." But when there is no more
room for expansion, artificial competition between state owned
corporations becomes the mode of economic stimulation. To McLeod
such a situation is a kind of cannibalism in which bureaucracies
begin to eat themselves.

The tragedy is that McLeod, like Red Valsen in The Naked and
the Dead, knows how the system works but can do nothing about it.
All he can do is speculate about a future which holds out the pros-
pect of forced labor to those who dare oppose it. "The bureaucrat
becomes driven to express his personality through anti-social
action," McLeod says, obviously thinking of his own life.

The conclusion that Mailer draws about what will happen once
there is no more room for expansion is the same one that Aldous
Huxley drew in Brave New World: that systems must clash and war will
be permanent. For war would be the only effective means of consump-
tion, the only way to avoid total impoverishment. Thus, one war would
end, new allies would be chosen, and war would begin again.

To avoid such a fate McLeod offers a solution, a way to break
the dialectical chain he has portrayed. He calls this solution
"revolutionary socialism." In this system, "the multiple" owns
and controls production and each person works, as in Marx's system,
"according to his ability and each is supplied according to his needs."

But such a revolution could be accomplished only if the people
are made aware of what is happening to them. As a literary artist,
that is Lovett's role in the novel. For it is the artist who makes
the people aware. To accomplish this goal the artist must portray

present conditions. Unlike the journalist, however, he must dis-
tort those conditions, metamorphose them into a prophecy of the
future. And this means the end of naturalism and realism in art,
for man is no longer in conflict with indifferent nature, but with
a dynamic society which is hostile to man's potential. No longer
can the artist be content to describe things the way they are, or,
rather, seem, because now the artist must show what the conditions
of society may eventually lead to.

Lovett is not sure the future McLeod predicts is valid until
Guinevere convinces him: she tells him that Monina is only a burden to her, an object that prevents her from totally abandoning herself to sensual pleasure. With this revelation Lovett sees a vision
of the hell McLeod describes. So he makes his preparations to act.
He pawns his typewriter and sends his novel to himself in care of
general delivery, under a new name. Then he asks McLeod for the
"little object," and McLeod gives him an envelope. When Hollingsworth
learns that the "little object" has escaped him he kills McLeod and
forces Guinevere and Monina to flee with him.

The envelope contained McLeod's will:

To Michael Lovett to whom, at the end of my life and for
the first time within it, I find myself capable of the
rudiments of selfless friendship, I bequeath in heritage
the remnants of my socialist culture.

Almost an afterthought he had scrawled:

And may he be alive to see the rising of the Phoenix.

So the heritage passed on to me, poor hope, and the little

object as well, and I went out into the world. If I fled

down the alley which led from that rooming house, it was

only to enter another, and then another . . . Thus, time

passes, and I work and I study, and I keep my eye on the

door.

Meanwhile, vast armies mount themselves, the world

revolves, the traveller clutches his breast. [p.223]

So what is that "little object?" Well, McLeod is correct when

he sometimes claims to have it and sometimes claims he does not. He

does give it to Lovett. He gives him the only way to survive in a

bureaucratic world. McLeod has left Lovett his heritage, his dream,

his inspiration. The key to it all is found in McLeod's name and

in his curious speech habit of dropping his "y's." For example, he

says "m'self," instead of "myself." So when the "y" is placed

back into William McLeod, it comes out "Will him my cloud." Thus,

Mailer suggests that Lovett has been left McLeod's heritage, his

individuality and hope for the future. The removal of individuality

and hope had disturbed the bureaucracy McLeod worked for, their loss

had removed the impetus from the revolution McLeod hoped to lead.

And because Hollingsworth had failed to achieve them, he was left

absolutely powerless.

So Lovett has learned that despair sets in when a man lives

only for the present, as his own psychological circumstances had

made him do. Lovett has learned that there is something superior

to narcissism, to living, that is, only for the present. He has

learned the existential lesson that what defines man and gives him

true autonomy and power is his awareness that not only will there
be a future if he works for it, but that by doing so he can help
to determine it. In Lovett's case, acting to effect the future
means two things: writing novels that are prophecies, and continuing to guard the awareness and inspiration that he has achieved
through his contact with McLeod. So he mails his novel to his new
name: he can drop his old one, the one he gave himself after his
amnesia. In doing so he drops the self-defeating narcissism of
living in the present. His old name was Mikey Lovett ("My key,
love it.") But in his will McLeod had addressed Mikey as Michael
Lovett ("Mike, he'll love it,") his name in the future. What Lovett
receives from McLeod, then, is not simply the idea that the older
revolutionary's doctrine may some day be realized, but the hope of
a better future. And it is that hope that forces the writer into
what Mailer recognizes as an existential awareness.

Chapter III Notes

[1]Norman Mailer, <u>Advertisements for Myself</u> (New York, G.P. Putnam's Sons, 1959), p. 188.

[2]Norman Mailer, <u>Barbary Shore</u> (New York, New American Library, 1951), p.43. [All subsequent citations are to this edition and are given in brackets].

[3]Norman Mailer, <u>Cannibals and Christians</u> (New York, Dell, 1966), pp. 238-239.

[4]<u>Cannibals and Christians</u>, pp.3-4.

[5]<u>Cannibals and Christians</u>, p. 80.

[6]<u>Cannibals and Christians</u>, p.3.

Chapter IV

The Deer Perk

The name, The Deer Park, comes from Mouffle D'Angerville's
Vie Privee De Louis XV: ou principaux evenements, particularités
et anecdotes de son regne, which describes the private sex resort,
called the Deer Park, maintained by the king.

In Advertisements for Myself, Mailer wrote that he originally
conceived of The Deer Park as part of an eight part novel,

> . . . the prologue to be the day of a small frustrated man,
> a minor artist manqué. The eight parts were to be eight
> stages of his dream later that night, and the books would
> revolve around the adventures of a mythical hero, Sergius
> O'Shaugnessy, who would travel through many worlds, through
> pleasure, business, communism, church, working class, crime,
> homosexuality and mysticism. To thicken the scheme, I was
> going to twist and scatter time, having many of the characters
> reappear in different books, but with their ages altered.
> Eitel and Elana, for example, would be forty-five and twenty-
> five in The Deer Park, and Sergius would be twenty-three,
> but later in the working class novel, Elena would be a girl
> of seventeen having her first affair with Sergius whose age
> would have come from twenty-three to forty. So the past
> for one would be the future of another.[1]

This idea was dropped after the first draft of The Deer Park.

The only other thing that remained was the prologue, called "The Man Who Studied Yoga." It is about a man, Sam Slavoda, middle-aged and average, who wishes to write a novel. He writes a comic strip for a living. His thoughts and his conversations with his wife are full of the phrases that his psychoanalist uses. When a few of his friends come over to view a pornographic movie, something none of them have ever done before, Sam hopes for an orgy. As they watch, each of them identifies with the people on the screen, but when the film is over all they do is talk about it in the same psychoanalist's jargon that Sam uses when alone with his wife.

There are other incidents in "The Man Who Studied Yoga" which likewise demonstrate Mailer's premise that people too often theorize about emotions rather than experience them, and that too often their theories are generations behind their actions or their desires for action. Mailer dropped "The Man Who Studied Yoga" as the prologue of The Deer Park, but he retained the theme of the story. The final draft of The Deer Park became for Mailer a proving-ground for his premise that theorization of emotion and life is a part of the American post World War II commercialism, a commercialism that has meant that "the mode by which we perceive reality can indeed become our reality."[2] In The Deer Park, Mailer argues that the theorization of emotion and life rather than genuine action is the basis for the life Americans now lead, a life of superficial and shallow thought of the type found in contemporary tooth paste advertisements and motion pictures. It is Mailer's overriding contention in The Deer Park that most people live not in reality, but in a dream of reality

which has been created by mass media and public relations groups.
And even the people who create those dreams--the movie makers,
statesmen, business men, and educators--do not control their creation.

Yet there are some people who are able to perceive the dream
and to escape logic and programmed emotion and so to enter into
Mailer's version of reality. These people, says Mailer, can be
found in any social class but are more often found in the lower
classes. Mailer's label for them in the 1950's and early 1960's
was the hipster, white Negro, or existentialist. Commenting on
Barbary Shore in Advertisements for Myself, Mailer said,

> For now, what can be underlined is that the direction
> I took in Barbary Shore was a first step toward work
> I will probably be doing from now on. For I wish to
> attempt an entrance into the mysteries of murder, su-
> icide, incest, orgy, orgasm, and Time. These themes
> now fill my head and make me think I have a fair chance
> to become the first philosopher of Hip.[3]

This new direction, Mailer reaffirmed many years later in Cannibals
and Christians, was brought about by modern society and the conditions for life that society offers:

> . . . the modern condition may be psychically so bleak,
> so plastic . . . that studies of loneliness, silence,
> corruption, orgy, and death can give life, can give a
> sentiment of beauty.[4]

The kind of character Mailer invented (though, by no means, in
a vacuum) to guide the reader through such studies was first introduced

in his essay, "The White Negro." That essay began with Mailer's comments on the then popular theme of despair over the possibility of mass death which this century offers. For Mailer, the greatest horror of mass death is its indignity. Even the threat of mass death causes widespread anxiety and a feeling that the individual's life has no meaning.

> . . . and so if in the midst of civilization—that civ-
> ilization founded upon the Faustian urge to dominate
> nature by mastering time, mastering the links of social
> cause and effect—in the middle of an economic civilization
> founded upon the confidence that time could indeed be
> subjected to our will, our psyche was subjected itself to
> the intolerable anxiety that death being causeless, life
> was causeless as well, and time deprived of cause and
> effect has come to a stop.[5]

In The Naked and the Dead, Mailer demonstrated this point of view in the scenes where the men find the dead Japanese corpses. Mailer argued that because of a "collective failure of nerve"—as when the men were powerless to prevent Croft from making them climb the mountain—men may never again see such a civilization as that so-called Faustian one which ended with World War II.

> It is on this bleak scene that a phenomenon has ap-
> peared: the American existentialist—the hipster, the
> man who knows that if our collective condition is to live
> with instant death by atomic war, relatively quick death
> by the State as l'univers concentrationaire, or with the

slow death by conformity with every creative and rebellious instinct stifled . . . why then the only
life-giving answer is to accept the terms of death,
to live with death as immediate danger, to divorce
oneself from society, to exist without roots, to set
out on that uncharted journey with the rebellious im-
peratives of the self. In short, whether the life is
criminal or not, the decision is to encourage the psychopath in oneself, to explore that domain of experience
where security is boredom and therefore sickness, and
one exists in the present, in that enormous present which
is without past or future, memory or planned intention,
the life where a man must go until he is beat, where he
must gamble with his energies through all those small or
large crises of courage and unforeseen situations which
beset his day, where he must be with it or doomed not to
swing.[6]

According to Mailer the archetype hipster "is the Negro for he has been
living on the margin between totalitarianism and democracy for two
centuries." But not all Negroes qualify as Mailer's archetypes, of
course, merely those who have learned to flourish by trusting their
paranoia, those who have learned to live for the "enormous present,"
"relinquishing the pleasures of the mind for the more obligatory
pleasures of the body." Mailer uses this mythical Negro as archetype
because, he says, as a member of an oppressed minority group, the
Negro's perception of the existential position is so acute:

What characterizes a member of a minority group is that
he is forced to see himself as both exceptional and in-
significant, marvelous and awful, good and evil. So far
as he listens to the world outside he is in danger of going insane. The only way he may relieve the unendurable
tension which surrounds any sense of his own identity is
to define his nature by his own acts; to discover his
courage or cowardice by actions which engage his courage;
discover his judgement by judging; his loyalty by being
tested; his originality by creating.[7]

This mode of living, says Mailer, was picked up by a few adventurous
city-dwelling Caucasions

who drifted out at night looking for action with a black
man's code to fit their facts. The hipster had absorbed
the existentialist synapses of the Negro, and for practical
purposes could be considered a white Negro.

To be an existentialist, one must be able to feel one-
self--one must know one's desires, one's rages, one's
anguish, one must be aware of the character of one's frustration and know what would satisfy it.[8]

In short, the hipster is a type of self-controlled psychopath. He must
exist in a state of perpetual anxiety in order to learn, for "one only
learns from situations in which the end is not known."[9] On the personality of the hipster Mailer quotes from his old friend Robert Linder,
a man whose ideas in great part shaped Mailer's own speculations during
that period.

The late Robert Linder, one of the few experts on
the subject, in his book, Rebel Without a Cause--The
Hypnoanalysis of a Criminal Psychopath presented part of
his definition in this way: the psychopath is a rebel
without a cause, an agitator without a program: in other
words, his rebelliousness is aimed to achieve goals
satisfactory to himself alone; he is incapable of ex-
ertions for the sake of others. All his efforts, hidden
under no matter what disguise, represent investments de-
signed to satisfy his immediate wishes and desires . . . .
Like a red thread the predominance of this mechanism
for immediate satisfaction runs through the history of
every psychopath. It explains not only his behavior but
also the violent nature of his acts.[10]

But Mailer, in commenting on this excerpt, goes on to assert that the
psychopath is really the admittedly dangerous forerunner of a personality type he expects to become the "central expression of human
nature before the twentieth century is over." As a matter of fact,
Mailer saw it emerging more and more in many executive and professional
people. Mailer's American existentialist lives in a world, by conscious
choice, of infantile fantasy. He strives, says Mailer, for love.
"Not love as the search for a mate, but love as the search for an
orgasm more apocalyptic than the one which preceded it." That is,
the emphasis is not upon the thing itself, but on the striving for it.
What separates the American existentialist from the criminal psychopath is that the former, "like children . . . [is] fighting for the

sweet." What separates him from the narcissist is that he is always
unsatisfied. For him, "movement is always to be preferred to in-
action." The quest, Mailer is quick to suggest, is akin to the quest
for the Holy Grail, and much involved with becomeing attuned to the
rhythm of life. This attuning is attained by liberating oneself from
what Mailer calls the "Super-ego of Society." In short, it is an
attempt to know oneself through immoderation. This is a new approach
for Mailer, a different direction from the one Mikey Lovett took.
Lovett had hoped for a chance to effect a change in society; Mailer's
hipster or existentialist knows that one cannot do more than change
oneself in order to live and flourish freely in a society too amorphous to be controlled. In The Deer Park, Sergius O'Shaugnessy tries
to do that.

The world Sergius moves in, though based upon a real model (Palm
Springs, California) is a surrealistic world in which reality is
juxtaposed with dream. Even the name of the resort is artificial,
for it is a perversion of Desert Door, the name it was given by the
early gold prospectors. Now the resort is an artificial oasis of
self love. There is no past and subsequently no future: "Everything is in the present tense." Nothing appears to be what it really
is, everything is disguised to look like something else.

It was a town built out of no other obvious motive
than commercial profit and so no sign of commerce was
allowed to appear. Desert D'Or was without a main
street, and its stores looked like anything but stores.
In those places which sold clothing no clothing was laid

out. . . There was a jewelery store built like a cabin
cruiser . . . .[11]

Just as Sinclair Lewis did in his opening paragraphs of Babbitt,
Mailer used the descriptions of the buildings to foreshadow his
character portrayals. Thus, the buildings in Babbitt were ". . .
frankly and beautifully office-buildings."[12] And the people in
Babbitt were frankly business people. The people of The Deer
Park, like the shops of Desert D'Or, hide their commercial motives
behind the veneer and facade of their artificial emotions. And it is
in this respect that Desert D'Or becomes a symbol for post World
War II America.

But there is another setting in the novel, a very important one.
As Howard Harper points out, this is Washington, the Washington of
the McCarthy era. The Deer Park is in part the story of the House
Un-American Activities Committee's harassment of the entertainment
industry. Thus, like Barbary Shore, The Deer Park continues to
trace the insidiousness of totalitarianism. Washington, on the
surface quite unlike Hollywood, is "still the other pole defining
the illusory world of The Deer Park."[13]

In his earlier novels, Mailer contended that in the type of power
structure that emerged out of the Second World War nobody really has
been able to control the flow of power, either personal or public.
In The Deer Park, Mailer concentrates mostly on one source of personal power, namely human sexuality and pleasure. He does so in
order to speculate upon how the post war perversion of that sexuality has made it almost impossible for any individual to achieve

personal power. Thus, Mailer seems to mean the setting of The
Deer Park not as a symbol for sexual power but as a metaphor for
the unexamined lust for commercial success that most people are
trying to satisfy, a lust which in great part has displaced normal
human sexuality and created a whole new life style. This new life
style is exploited by the business world through the use of what
Mailer labeled in Cannibals and Christians a kind of subconscious
pornography. "You get enormously attractive girls selling cigar-
ettes, which is a perversion of sex because an enormously attractive
girl should be presented for what she is, and not as a handmaiden to
a little box containing some paper, tobacco, and cellophane."[14]
The Deer Park, then, is really an extrapolation of the themes defined
in Mailer's first two novels. He shows in The Deer Park that he
still believes his earlier predictions of the future, the ones he
made through General Cummings in The Naked and the Dead and McLeod
in Barbary Shore, were more or less accurate. But it was not until
many years later, when he came to write The Prisoner of Sex, that
Mailer, in re-thinking these concepts, came to feel that their historical roots went beyond America and stretched down into the Renaissance, the first age to exhalt man over God.

The Deer Park, then, is a sociological adventure story, a
modern venture into vanity and the subsequent human failures it
implies. Mailer traced these themes through the eyes of Sergius
O'Shaugnessy, an outsider who witnesses the Deer Park that is Desert
D'Or and for a while participates in its illusion. Sergius, an
ex-Air Force flier, describes himself in the metaphor of an actor.

As the plot unfolds it becomes apparent that he is just that, an
actor in life looking for his role. Like Mikey Lovett of <u>Barbary</u>
<u>Shore</u>, Sergius does not know his real name. Sergius is merely a
"stage name." His father made it up when he left Sergius at an
orphanage. Sergius was given a medical discharge from the Air
Force after a small mental breakdown which he suffered after seeing in
an orpahanage hospital some of the children upon whom he had dropped
napalm.

So after mysteriously winning fourteen thousand dollars in a
crap game he went to Desert D'Or to gain experience and to learn to
write. But he needed a guide because he was becoming too fascinated
with the lust for power and prestige he saw around him. Only two
people qualify as mentors for him, and even they qualify only in part.
The first, Marion Faye, is the son of ex-gossip columnist Dorothea
O'Faye. The illegitimate son of a prince, he is a pimp. The name
O'Fay suggests "OFAY," the then current Negro term for Caucasians
by way of Pig-Latin. But as a boy Marion had dropped the "O" from
his last name. Marion's appearance and actions are those of Mailer's
white Negro. In addition, his name has overtones of Morgan le Fay.
Marion is an apprentice hipster, living like Balzac's Gobseck in the
belief that only self-preservation and promotion are important.
Sergius relates that Marion Faye likes him because, "I had killed
people, I had almost killed myself, and these were emotions he considered interesting." In other words, Faye sees Sergius as a potential
hipster.

The second person Sergius meets is Faye's friend, Charles Francis

Eitel, the film director. His name is pronounced EYEtel--C.F. EYE-
tel; the big question about him is whether he will cooperate with
the Senate Un-American Activities Committee (see if I tell). So
far he has not, and Sergius is very impressed by Eitel's political
courage. The director is a vanishing breed: the courageous hero
of the pre-World War II mold. But as the novel unfolds, Eitel's
courage fades into caution and from caution to cowardice. At the
same time he moves from passion to technique, from compassion to
guilt, from guilt to anxiety, from anxiety to greed. His life becomes the game he loves to play so much, charades. Of him Marion
Faye says, "very nineteenth century, you know." In the beginning
he does represent all the virtues of that century. His degeneration
is symbolic of the worldwide degeneration of the values he embodies.

Eitel does not cooperate with the subcommittee and is black-
listed. At first he sees this fate as an opportunity to make finally
the commitment to create an artistic motion picture instead of the
shallow commercial films he has been directing. He also sees his
blacklisting as an opportunity to spend more time with his mistress,
Elena, and to become closer to her emotionally. In both his films
and his lovemaking he has been for years a devotee of mere technique
and of nothing else. Now he can "escape the institution," as Mikey
Lovett had put it in Barbary Shore. In Eitel's case it is the institution of the Deer Park, where everything is illusion and all a
person is required to do is copy the illusion faithfully.

When he returns to Desert D'Or from Washington, Eitel is am-
bivalent about what he has done. His indecision over whether to

choose autonomy over power is shown in a scene in which he sees a
girl on the beach and desires to make love to her and to learn to
surf. Eitel daydreams for a while, then realizes he no longer has
his fame, influence, or youth with which to interest the girl. So
he moves off. When Eitel describes the above to Sergius, the would-
be writer becomes confused:

> I had the idea that there were two worlds. There was
> a real world as I called it, a world of wars and boxing
> clubs and children's homes on back streets, and this
> real world was a world where orphans burned orphans.
> It was better not even to think of this. I liked the
> other world in which everybody lived. The imaginary
> world. [p.47]

At a party in which, in a kind of grotesque parody of the power
ladder of The Naked and the Dead, the various rungs of the Hollywood
power structure divide according to rank, Eitel meets Elena and begins
his attempt at a commitment to love. Sergius meets the movie star,
and a former wife of Eitel, Lulu Meyers. Later in the evening, thanks
to her lovemaking technique, Sergius regains the potency he had lost
when he had his nervous breakdown. But he confuses his sexual appetites
with love. So he makes his entrance into the surface world of the
Deer Park, where technique counts more than emotion. Sergius describes
his plight of having to choose either the commercial world of power or
the artist's world of autonomy in this manner:

> Quite a few times I have thought that a newspaperman
> is obsessed with finding the facts in order to tell a

> lie, and a novelist is a gelley-slave to his imagination
>
> so he can look for the truth. [p.100]

Meanwhile, Eitel has become deeply involved with Elena and she
soon becomes his inspiration for autonomy. He begins to think about
the reasons he had begun to make commercially rather than artistically
acceptable films and realizes his youthful rage has mellowed into wit,
his talent diverted and spent in the process. But now Eitel feels he
is free from the commercial institution and so he writes an outline for
an artistic movie.

While Eitel gropes toward art Sergius moves away from it. He
is too busy enjoying his new found power with Lulu, or rather his
illusion of power. He describes it in the following manner:

> Poor millions with their low roar! They would never
>
> have what I had now. They could shiver outside, make
>
> a shrine in their office desk or on the shelf of their
>
> olive-drab lockers, they could look at the pin-up picture
>
> of Lulu Meyers. I knew I was good when I carried a
>
> million men on my shoulder. [p.130]

The preceeding passage is a hint at what is Sergius' major block toward
"hip;" his narcissism is too intellectual, and it is leading him
deeper and deeper down the Wonderland path of illusion. This is no
better shown than in the following passage in which he describes his
affair.

> We played our games. I was the photographer and she was
>
> the model; she was the movie star and I was the bellhop;

> she did the queen, I the slave. We even met even
> to even. The game she loved was to play the bobby-
> soxer who sat with a date in the living room and was
> finally convinced, always for the first time naturally
> enough. She was never so happy as when we acted at
> theater and did the mime on clouds of myth. [p.138]

Here Sergius is at the furthest pole from reality that he reaches
in the novel; he is playing life rather than living it. What he
thinks of as love is really peer-group pressure. He is aware of
the pressure but refuses to admit the reality of his own words.
If he has achieved a kind of intellectual narcissism, he has not
been able to turn it into effective existential action.

Marion Faye's problem is exactly the opposite. He has achieved
the physical discipline of the non-criminal psychopath but cannot achieve
the intellectual narcissism that will allow him to rid himself of the
feeling of guilt that accompanies his lack of compassion. He is
able to take extra money from one of his call girls without much
guilt, but after Paco, a narcotics addict, begs him for either money
or a "fix," and he tells him to go and knock over a store, Faye
feels so guilty about it that he cannot sleep. He tries to reason
himself out of guilt by convincing himself that compassion is not
only the "queen to guilt," but also a vice to be shed. Yet his logic
does not alleviate his insomnia and so he finally gets up and takes
a long fast ride in his car to ease his nerves. As the sun comes up
it dawns on him why he must banish guilt.

Faye remembered a time when he gambled around the clock,

78

not even pausing at dawn when a great light, no more
than when a shadow of the original blast somewhere
further in the desert, had dazzled the gaming rooms
and lit with an illumination colder than the neon
tube above the green roulette cloth the harsh dead
faces of the gamblers who had worn their way through
the night.

Even then there were factories out there, out somewhere in the desert, and the tons of ore all in the
freight cars were being shuttled into the great mouth,
and the factory labored, it labored like a gambler
for twenty-four hours of the day, reducing the mountain
of earth to a cup of destruction, and it was even possible that at this moment soldiers were filing into
trenches a few miles from a loaded tower, and there they
would wait, cowering in the dawn, while army officers
explained their purposes in the words of newspaper stories,
for the words belonged to the slobs, and the slobs hid

the world with words. [pp.160-161]

Keeping in mind what Sergius had said about newspapers, the
reader realizes that if Faye is to achieve any existential freedom
in a world so threatened by the dehumanization of mass death he must
develop an intellectual narcissism as powerful as the detachment from
compassion that he has already achieved. And Faye himself knows that
he cannot live "hip" unless he can achieve the psychopathy of guilt-
lessness.

Meanwhile, Eitel's movement toward "hip," like his would-be masterpiece, is turning out, by his own admission, poorly. He is beginning to realize that he does not have the integrity of the artist to do nothing but his best. Eitel's output becomes smaller and its quality poorer until Herman Teppis' son-in-law inspires him to turn it into a commercial work, to fill it with the kind of things that people want to hear. He does this and soon the work is flowing quickly again. It is at this time that he also decides he wants to direct the movie he is writing. In order to do that he knows he will have to cooperate with the Senate Un-American Activities Committee.

Then Sergius is offered another temptation to power in the form of twenty thousand dollars. The money is offered by the motion picture studio for the rights to film his real-life adventures as an air ace, a life story which has already undergone major "improvements." The movie men need Sergius because they know that without some foundation in reality the story would seem unreal even by Hollywood standards. But Sergius realizes they are trying to turn his rather degrading past into a story of sentimental heroics. He does not want to be that kind of false hero. Sergius knows that in order to achieve his goals he must achieve more than intellectual narcissism; he must perfect his controlled non-criminal psychopathy, or what Mailer calls "the cruelty to be a man."

When actor Teddy Pope and comedian Tony Tanner begin to join Sergius and Lulu on their evenings out, Sergius observes their behavior and learns from his observations that like everyone else in the Deer Park, he is himself searching for personal integrity, for "a moment of integrity." But Sergius still cannot distinguish between integrity and morality, and the illusion of integrity and morality, even when Lulu confesses to him that,

> "I slept with Tony Tanner."

> "But where? When?" I cried aloud, as if to learn what was most important of all.

> "In a phone booth." [p.238]

Sergius cannot yet recognize the disparity between Lulu's moral sounding euphemism, "slept with," and her utterly depraved act. There are other such illusions and confusions in Desert D'Or, as, for example, when Elena, Eitel's mistress, wants to become a nun. She wants to do so because "a nun is never alone." She confuses love with security.

Another such illusion is Lulu's equating human understanding with a kind of Machiavellianism, as when she says to Eitel that "I've always thought it's the people who can hurt you who understand you best." This is a natural reaction for an inhabitant of a deer park, a place where personal gain is always thought of as being at the expense of someone else's personal loss. There is no real power in Hollywood, merely an illusion of power. Gossip columnists such as Dorothea O'Faye are powerful only because people believe that what they write is important. Movie stars are powerful only because others believe them worthy of adoration. And so upon a false assumption, illusion is built upon illusion until even the illusion builders scare themselves with their false notions of power, and the Bimmler ratings, which list each actor's current popularity, becomes the measure of success, status, and power. Eitel recognizes the illusion:

> The essence of spirit, he thought to himself, was to
> choose the thing which did not better one's position
> but made it more perilous. That was why the world he
> knew was poor, for it insisted morality and caution
> were identical.[p.257]

And yet, in the end, when he consciously chooses caution, he, too, fools himself into believing that caution and morality are the same. So the people of The Deer Park, like the older waiter in Hemingway's "A Clean, Well Lighted Place," pay homage to an empty thing, a machine. For the waiter it was a small cup at the altar of a coffee urn, and for the people of The Deer Park it is the ritual of commercialism. And this Sergius sees in the closing hours of a party at Dorothea O'Faye Pelly's house.

> . . . the drunk at the one-armed bandit who dropped quarter
> after quarter in a solemn, rhythmic way seemed to have become
> the gambler turned inside out, showing in contrast to his sober
> passion that he could dominate the machine, the knowledge that
> now he merely fed it in homage, and seemed never so surprised
> as when occasionally the box gave back some coins with a clatter.
> [p.259]

For Lulu the ultimate reward of life is the adoration of her fans. For Herman Teppis, the head of the studio, it is the material rewards his own personal God gathers for him. In one of the most humorous chapters of the book Teppis tries to marry Lulu to the homosexual Teddy Pope in order to bolster their respective Bimmler ratings. His office is a perfect setting for the scene of his procrustian stretch of morality.

It was an enormous room with an enormous picture window, and
the main piece of furniture was the desk, a big old Italian
antique which had come down from the Vatican. Yet, like an
old house which is made over so completely that only the shell
remains, the inside of Teppis' desk was given to a noiseless
tape recorder, a private file, and a small revolving bar. [p.263]

First he sets Teddy up by feeding him spoonfuls of sentiment. Teppis
asks him,

". . . What do you need to be successful here?"

"Heart," said Teddy.

"That's right, a big red heart. The American public has
a big heart and you got to meet it, you got to go halfway up
to it." [p.265]

He dismisses Teddy and brings Lulu into his office. The reader finds
out just how far power morality has come since General Cummings' musings
about it during the Second World War when Teppis makes his final appeal
to her to marry Pope.

". . . Lulu, listen to me. The trouble is you're weak,
publicity wise."

"I've got the best press agent in the country," she said
quickly.

"You think you can buy good publicity? Good publicity is a
gift of God. The time is past, Lulu, when any sort of girl,
you'll see I'm speaking frankly, the kind of girl who's so-called
friends with this man and friends with that man until she's notorious.

The public wants what's respectible today. You know why?
Life ain't respectable any more. Think they want to be
reminded of that? Let me show you psychology. Ten years
ago, a woman she was faithful, she wanted excitement, she
wanted to dream she was having a big affair with a star.
. . . Today . . . that same woman she has boyfriends all
over the place, with the man who fixes the television set,
people like that. You think she wants to see somebody just
like herself on the screen, somebody just as nuts as she is?
She don't. She's ashamed of herself. She wants to see a
woman she can respect, a married woman, a royal couple, the
Number One married lovers of America . . . ." [p.273]

And so the bounderies of the deer park are bigger than Hollywood
and Desert D'Or. They stretch over all America. But to Lulu the illusion
is still intact.

Tears ran down her cheeks. "H.T., I want to get
married," she said in a tremulous voice. "I want to
love just one man and have a beautiful mature relationship and have beautiful children and be a credit to the
industry." [p.276]

Meanwhile, Sergius is becoming more aware of what has been blocking
his attempt to become "hip." This awareness comes about as a result of
the terror tactics of the burly special investigators for the Senate Un-
American Activities Committee, who pay Sergius a visit. When they leave
he thinks of himself as having been the "patsy for the world." He is
in much the same marginal position at that point as Mailer said the

American Negro was in his essay, "The White Negro." But Sergius, like all of Mailer's heroes, must first undergo an extensive training period at the local library if he is ever going to "speak up to the rough world out there." So he reads twelve hours a day.

Sergius still thinks of Eitel as his mentor, only he has grown larger than his teacher and so can only think that the things he discovers for himself are the whisperings of Eitel. Among these whisperings are Sergius' realization that hedonism will prevent his accomplishing what he wants to do. As an artist he feels he must shun the world of the imagination and

> "try for that other world, the real world, where orphans burn orphans and nothing is more difficult to discover than a simple fact. And with that pride of the artist, you must blow against the wall of every power that exists, the small trumpet of your defiance." [p.374]

So Sergius has entered into the fringe of "hip." He knows the value of his body, saying, ". . . a good time is what gives us the strength to try again." He is ready to explore the mysteries of time and orgy.

> There are hours when I have the arrogance to reply to the Lord Himself, and so I ask, "Would You agree that sex is where philosophy begins?"
>
> But God, who is the oldest of the philosphers, answers in His weary cryptic way, "Rather think of Sex as Time, and Time as the connection of new circuits." [p.375]

Mailer offered some insight into this rather cryptic statement some years later, in Cannibals and Christians:

> Think of [the] Devil as the echo of history, the lore of
> the past, the mansions of philosophy, as the blunt weight
> of every problem which has succeeded. Think of this Devil
> as the spirit of magic and the dead spirit of institutional
> life, as mass communication, and the passing of the guards.
> . . . So take Spirit and pose it upon the Vision of the
> future--between just these two leviathans, at their junction,
> is moral nature. Of course this moral nature, this junction,
> is being rotted by the plague.[15]

Sergius is now free to search for the reality he could not find in
Hollywood or even in Mexico. What he has learned is that the mores
and moral restraints that used to be in force before, say, World War
II, no longer seem as inhibiting to most people any more. Thus, people
may pay lip service to the values of old but seek, and are driven, by
new and hitherto unknown ones. Mailer, in The Deer Park, is seeking
to identify those new values and a hero who can cope with them.

The implication for Mailer's art, as Norman Podhoretz points out,
is that "for the first time . . . victory over the system is possible
to those who see through it and are sufficiently brave to act on what
they see."[16] In The Deer Park, none of the characters has achieved
that ultimate victory. Sergius is close, but it would take another
hundred or so pages for him to really achieve it.

Chapter IV Notes

[1]Advertisements for Myself, p.143.

[2]Existential Errands (New York, 1972), p.77.

[3]Advertisements for Myself, p.99.

[4]Cannibals and Christians(New York, 1966), p.269.

[5]Advertisements for Myself, p.312.

[6]Advertisements for Myself, pp. 312-313.

[7]Cannibals and Christians, p.77.

[8]Advertisements for Myself, p.315.

[9]"Responses and Reactions," IV The Presidential Papers (New York, 1963),p.197.

[10]Advertisemtns for Myself, p.318

[11]Norman Mailer, The Deer Park (New York, 1955), p.3. All subsequent citations are to this edition and are given within brackets.

[12]Babbitt (New York, 1922), p.1.

[13]Howard M. Harper, Jr., Desperate Faith: A Study of Salinger, Mailer, Baldwin, and Updike (Chapel Hill, North Carolina),p. 196.

[14]Cannibals and Christians, p. 196.

[15]Cannibals and Christians, p. 366.

[16]"Norman Mailer: The Embattled Vision," Partisan Review, XXVI (Summer, 1959), 386.

Chapter V

An American Dream

An American Dream is not a surrealistic work; Mailer rejects the
Freudian base of surrealism. But, in Mailer's canon, An American Dream
is unique. It is a tale of dreamlike proportions based upon an existentialist theology that attributes to man a share of the power of
both God and the devil, the two warring factions, as Mailer sees them,
of the universe. It shows how one man becomes aware of that struggle
in the universe, and in himself. As noted above, in chapter IV, Mailer
had written about this idea in an essay contained in Cannibals and
Christians. He reiterated it some years later in The Presidential
Papers:

> If God is not all-powerful but existential, discovering
> the possibilities and limitations of His creative powers
> in the form of the history which is made by His creatures,
> then one must postulate an existential equal to God, an
> antagonist, the Devil, a principle of Evil whose signature
> was the concentration camps, whose joy is to waste substance,
> whose intent is to prevent God's conception of Being from
> reaching its mysterious goal. If one considers the hy-
> pothesis that God is not all powerful, but rather, the
> creator of Nature, then evil becomes a record of the Devil's
> victories over God.[1]

Thus, man's role, as Mailer has written in Advertisements For Myself, is profoundly elevated:

> we are a part of--perhaps the most important part--of His
> great expression, His enormous destiny; perhaps He is
> trying to impose upon the universe His conception of be-
> ing against other conceptions of being very much opposed
> to His. Maybe we are in a sense the seed, the seed-car-
> riers, the voyagers, the explorers, the embodiment of
> that embattled vision; maybe we are engaged in a heroic
> activity, and not a mean one.[2]

An American Dream, then, represents in the symbolism of fiction the
ideas Mailer earlier presented in essays in which he explained his
idea of the newly emerging man, the "hipster," the psychopath, the
white Negro, and the existentialist. It is the task of Steven Rojack,
the hero and narrator of the book, to fight God's battle for Him and
with his own body and psyche by overcoming the American dreams, the
dreams projected by the lives and works of the players of the deer
park--

> the sexual dreams of Don Juan, the Alger dream of the
> self-made man, the outsider's dream of the inside, the
> Mafia's dream of money and power, the square's dream of
> the life of the hipster, the hipster's dream of death.[3]

Steven Rojack is such a dream figure. He is the embodiment of Mailer's
own version of the dream of power. Rojack is an ex-congressman, an
author (his book, The Psychology of the Hangman), an intellectual, a
war hero, a television talk show host, a boxer, a great lover, and
a university professor of "existentialist psychology with the not

inconsiderable thesis that magic, dread, and perception of death
were the roots of motivation."

Rojack inhabits a world manipulated by powers unknown to most
people except in dreams, in nightmares of intimation, that suggest
the understructure of society, the frame, the stage-top inhabited
by the string-pullers, the powerful politicians, industrialists,
mafia, and Pentagon chiefs, the demi-gods and devils whose roles
and duties often merge in one powerful man.

But there is another side to Rojack. It is represented by his
estranged wife, Deborah Mangaravidi Kelly, whom he met on a double
date with John F. Kennedy.

> She was Deborah Caughlin Mangaravidi Kelly, of the
> Caughlins first, the English-Irish Bankers, financiers
> and priests; the Mangaravidis, a Sicilian issue from the
> Bourbons and the Hapsburgs; Kelly's family was just
> Kelly; but he had made a million two hundred times. So
> there was a vision of treasure, far-off blood, and fear.[4]

In Rojack's description of Deborah is the suggestion that she is symbolic of the power-brokers that must be defeated in order to achieve
personal and metaphysical power and autonomy. Symbolically, too, is
the fact that Deborah has frequently been unfaithful to Steven. They
are living apart when the novel opens. Steven is quite shattered by
the experience of the separation and even contemplates suicide. He
has lost that part of his masculinity Mailer defined in Cannibals and
Christians as honor:

> When a man can't find any dignity in his work, he loses

virility. Masculinity is not something given to you,
something you're born with, but something you gain.
And you gain it by winning small battles with honor.
Because there is very little honor left in American
life, there is a certain built-in tendency to destroy
masculinity in American men.[5]

Rojack goes to visit his wife. When they are together, Deborah
tells him that at the moment she has three lovers, all of whom enjoy
her dexterity at anal intercourse, a perversion associated in Mailer's
theology with the devil because of its non-productive properties.
When Rojack mentions his own lovers, "a powerful odor of rot and
musk and something more violent came from her [his wife]. It was
like the scent of the carnivore in a zoo." This is the first of
what Phillip Rahv calls a "whole series of extravaganzas of the olfactory sense, a kind of olfactory mysticism, permitting Rojack to
smell what are really states of mind rather than states of the body."[6]
In Cannibals and Christians, Mailer himself put it this way:

. . . the secret emotions of one's being, the basic
emotions, courage and cowardice, betray their presence
in the odor [of one's excrement] and greed as well, or
cupidity, ambition, compassion, love, trust, tenderness,
savagery. The way in which we take souls from the food
is the mirror of the dirty ape [the id] inside. If most
of us abhor shit, it is because most of us are a little
hideous inside.[7]

Steven and Deborah argue. Finally he strangles her. Deborah's

death is the reawakening of both his sexual power and personal autonomy.
By having the courage to kill her, Rojack has become the existential
hero. According to Mailer, "courage can be found in men whose conflict is caught between their ambition and their cowardice."[8] By having
the courage to take the leap, so to speak, Rojack has a chance to
escape the American Dream and to join God's forces and fight to make
His ideas prevail. Thus, Mailer ends the first chapter of the novel.
Like Tolstoy's The Death of Ivan Ilyich, the climax of An American
Dream comes first; the rest of the novel is a record of Rojack's psychological and intellectual development.

In chapter two Rojack begins by explaining that Deborah was obsessed with the idea of Grace, a notion she attempted to impart to
him. He murdered her, freed himself of her theory of an omnipotent
God, and substituted his creator's thesis of an existential One.
With her death, Rojack has lost most of his dread. And he wants to
live.

He goes down the hall and into the other bedroom, where he finds
his wife's German maid, Ruta, masterbating. With the olfactory imagery that Rojack uses to describe her, it is apparent that she is
a personaification of Europe, an influence Rojack (America) must
slough off in order to achieve existential freedom. Rojack performs
anal intercourse with Ruta. Through this act Rojack says "a host of
the Devil's best gifts were finally coming to me, mendacity, guile,
a fine-edged cupidity for the stroke that steals, the wit to trick
authority." Rojack refuses the act of creation on such a one as
Ruta; he has begun to fight on God's side by abandoning the morality

of caution. He does so without any assurance that he will ever
be able to free himself from the forces of destruction and sodomy
(the devil) and find the force of love and creation (God). With
suprarealistic and erotic imagery Mailer has thus created

> . . . a radically moral book about radically immoral
>
> subjects, a religious book that transcends the con-
>
> ventional limits of blasphemy to expose the struggle
>
> toward psychic redemption that is the daily warfare
>
> of our secret outlaw selves.[9]

Convinced that he murdered Deborah, the police take Rojack in
for questioning but soon release him for lack of solid evidence.
Thus he is free to search for love. When he meets a nightclub singer,
Cherry, he believes he has a chance to achieve love. In describing
Rojack's and Cherry's lovemaking, Rojack says, "we paid our devotions
in some church no larger than ourselves." He is well aware at this
point of his existential responsibilities, of his "hip." So he in-
terrupts his intercourse with her. "I searched for that corporate
rubbery obstruction I detested so much, found it with a finger, pulled
it forth, flipped it away from the bed." His equating corporate enterprise with sterility links Rojack to the power structure Mailer described in all his previous novels. When they finish, Cherry admits
that Rojack has brought her to her first orgasm.

Mailer equates orgasm with the rage to power and, it will be
remembered, with the hipster's search for love. In The Prisoner of
Sex, Mailer will say:

> The Lord, Master of Existential Reason, was not thus

devoted to the absurd as to put the orgasm in the midst

of the act of creation without cause of the profoundest

sort, for when a man and woman conceive, would it not

be best that they be able to see one another for a trans-

cendent instant, as if the soul of what would then be

conceived might live with more light later?[10]

When Rojack leaves Cherry and goes back to his own apartment to get

dressed for his meeting with his father-in-law, he receives some phone

calls which seem at first to be bad news: he learns that his television

talk show has been cancelled and his university has asked him to take

a leave of absence. But with each call Rojack becomes more and more

free from the ladder of social power that General Cummings described

in The Naked and the Dead in which one fears those above and is feared

by those below. He is also freed from the stupefying institution of

bureaucracy Mikey Lovett escaped in Barbary Shore, and from the world

of illusions Mailer depicted in The Deer Park. But Rojack is still

not completely free. He must still meet with his father-in-law,

whom Rojack dreads.

In his commentary upon the Hasidic legend of Zusya, "The Fear of

God," Mailer gave a hint at the meaning of that fear Rojack felt. In

that essay Mailer defined it as the "fear God feels Himself" that in

creating man He did not conceive a being of stamina and nobility but

of sloth and treachery, and that therefore God's

ultimate victory over the Devil is no more uncertain

than the Devil's victory over God--either may conquer

man and so give Being a characteristic Good or Evil,

> or indeed each may exhaust the other, until Being
> 11
> ceases. . . .

When Cherry tells Rojack the story of Shago Martin, the hip Negro

singer, it reaffirms his belief that as long as he keeps his own

hip he cannot be defeated. He is now ready to discover who his

father-in-law really is, and to do battle with him if need be. Now

his mind begins to function on the symbolic level which to Mailer

is religion. His mind asks him to prove his courage in symbolic

ways, and to prove he is fighting for good rather than evil. And

yet as the taxi gets nearer to Kelly's suite at the Waldorf Rojack's

dread becomes more acute. Then suddenly he is free from the deer

park notion that morality is caution, and from the Cummings-McLeod

idea of a Leviathon morality. He has discovered the true source of

morality, as Mailer sees it.

> Men were afraid of murder, but not from a terror of
>
> justice so much as the knowledge that a killer at-
>
> tracted the attention of the gods; then your mind
>
> was not your own, your anxiety ceased to be neurotic,
>
> your dread was real. Omens were as tangible as bread.
>
> There was an architecture to eternity which housed us
>
> as we dreamed, and when there was a murder, a cry went
>
> through the market place of sleep. Eternity had been
>
> deprived of a room. [p.192]

And so Rojack goes up the elevator to see Kelly. His description

of the elevator ride as a descent into hell shows that he has been con-

vinced of Kelly's true identity. Kelly is a devil, an agent of Satan.

As he descends into hell, his mind tells him to go to Harlem to
find Shago Martin and fight with him for Cherry. He refuses this
symbolic act of sacrifice by trying to be rational about his caution,
even though he realizes that caution gives birth to the illusion of
reality which grows up only to smother love. Subsequently, he loses
Cherry. Rojack has yet to learn that full emotional and not mere
intellectual commitment to love is hip, or existential power, the
only kind possible in society as Mailer has defined it in his earlier
novels. In The Deer Park, Faye and Eitel failed to learn that lesson,
and Sergius was only beginning to learn it when the novel ended. But
in the next few chapters of An American Dream, Rojack does learn it.

When he gets to Kelly's hotel suite, the first thing he does is
see his step-daughter, Deirdre, who explains to him another reason
for his fear.

> "Mummy told me once that you were a young soul and
> she was an old one. There was the trouble . . . she had
> had other lives . . .But you are a new soul, she said,
> and hadn't had a life before this one. . . she had to go
> on to say you were a coward . . . People with new souls
> have a terror cause they can't know if they'll be born
> again." [p. 200]

In Cannibals and Christians, Mailer further illuminated this idea:

> A soul can lose its best qualities, its courage, its
> compassion, its grace, or it can slough off its worst
> features, its cowardice, its terror, its avarice, its
> sloth. A soul is changed by inhabiting a body. At the

time of its little death, it is better or it is worse
than when it entered that body. Its form has altered.[12]

Then Rojack goes in to see his father-in-law. Like General
Cummings, Kelly resembles any number of "generals, tycoons, politicians, newspaper publishers, presidents and prime ministers."
He represents the controlling forces of modern society. Because
there are other people in the room, Rojack goes out on the terrace
until they leave. It is there that his psyche asks of his body the
Christ sacrifice. His mind asks him to jump off the terrace and kill
himself in order to free the baby that Cherry is now carrying from
his (and symbolically, America's) sordid past. He cannot do it.

Finally, Rojack's father-in-law enters the room. He begins at
once to make his first, preliminary overtures to Rojack. The temp-
tations this devil offers Rojack are the same as those he offered to
Christ. Kelly tells Rojack he has been watched closely by both God
and the devil because he is a man of wealth and power. They vie for
his favor and exact revenge upon him just as Ares and Athena did with
the heroes of Ilium and Greece. The reason both warring parties are
so interested in him is that men at the top can influence God's or
the devil's destinies to a greater degree than ordinary people can.
Rojack knows that if he can defeat Kelly he will have won a major
victory for God and increased as well both his own autonomy and his
existential influence. He gets the opportunity to defeat Kelly when
the final confrontation occurs. Rojack admits he killed Deborah:

> "Yes, I killed her," I said, "but I didn't seduce her
> when she was fifteen, and never leave her alone, and

never end the affair." [p. 236]

The result of this incestuous union is Deirdre, the saint-like child. So by killing his demon-wife, and refusing to join forces with his father-in-law, Rojack has defeated both Kelly, the devil's solicitor, and defeated the evil outside of himself. Now he must defeat the evil within himself by overcoming his terror and so gaining existential power. He must perform the symbolic act of walking the parapet of Kelly's apartment terrace and thus free himself from fear.

So he does. He walks around the parapet of Kelly's terrace, which, appropriately, is forty feet across and forty stories up. He hears the voice of the moon, of Deborah, and feels the pull of sterility again, of evil, that is, telling him to jump. But he defeats his cowardice. The voice of the good forces, however, tells him that he must walk the parapet again. The first time was to save himself. The second time is to save Cherry. But Kelly tries to push him off, and so, fear overcoming him, he jumps back to the safety of the terrace and rushes off to see Cherry. By the time he reaches her she has been beaten up and soon dies on the ambulance stretcher. Rojack has freed himself from the institution but did not have the courage to free others. He slipped back into Eitel's morality of caution only for a moment and lost the reality that was Cherry.

There is an epilogue to the novel. In it, Rojack, driving on the open road toward the desert, stops off to see a doctor friend and to watch the autopsy of a man who had died of cancer. The man is symbolic of American post war society. When the stench of the rancid cells reaches him, Rojack discovers why man must achieve psychopathy or perish. If man denies his own rage and frustration and doesn't let it out, "it goes into tissues, is swallowed by the cells. The cells go mad. Cancer is the growth of madness denied."

With this idea still mulling, Rojack drives across the desert. He has not been overwhelmed by the power structure, but neither does he have any hope of reforming society, of pulling down the neon signs he sees glowing out of Las Vegas, which are symbolic of the post World War II illusory world. He has learned that the only one he can save is himself.

Rojack could have saved Cherry, the symbol of real love, says Mailer, by becoming "hip," either by going to Harlem and exposing himself to real dread, or by walking the parapet two times and so exposing himself artificially to dread. But Kelly, the symbol of the established power structure, prevents him from going around the second time. Because Rojack did not go to Harlem to achieve "hip" by facing dread, but instead attempted to usurp the hipster's power using the tactics of the power establishment, by beating up Shago Martin, the hipsters of Harlem killed Cherry. They took away Rojack's chance to achieve love. So Rojack is himself free, but he is alone. And now he must search for love again.

An American Dream, then, shows the attempt of one man to break away from that dream world which has become for too many people their real world. But more than this, An American Dream is an attempt to explain that if the old moral code were killed in World War II, morality itself remained a vital question with which the people living under the new power structure must reckon. It is Mailer's contention that although morality is no longer something from within, something acquired at

youth from one's parents as a guiding principle, morality is existential;

one's existential actions have metaphysical implications and physical

ones as well. That is, one's actions and thoughts have an effect upon

God and the devil, and also upon the body of the indiviual. One de-

termines God's fate with one's thoughts and actions along with the

fate of one's own cells, for cancer, Mailer surmises, is the result of

repressed violence and frustration.

Chapter V

Notes

[1]The Presidential Papers (New York, 1963), p.193.

[2]Advertisements for Myself, p.351.

[3]James Toback, "Norman Mailer Today," Commentary XLIV:4 (Oct. 1967), 73.

[4]Norman Mailer, An American Dream (New York, 1970), p.7. All subsequent citations are to this edition and are given in the text within brackets.

[5]Cannibals and Christians, p. 201.

[6]Phillip Rahv, "Crime Without Punishment," The New York Review of Books, IV (March 25, 1965), 4.

[7]Cannibals and Christians, p. 297.

[8]Existential Errands, p. 297.

[9]Brom Weber, "A Fear of Dying: Norman Mailer's An American Dream," The Hollins Critic II:3 (June, 1965), 5.

[10]The Prisoner of Sex (Boston, 1971), pp. 87-88.

[11]Cannibals and Christians, p. 377.

[12]Cannibals and Christians, p. 353.

Chapter VI

History As Novel As History:

Armies of the Night

Armies of the Night is a curious book. Though far from his best,
it is the only one yet to win the Pulitzer Prize and the National Book
Award. Both prizes were given, as prizes usually are, for reasons of
politics rather than aesthetics. Mailer took what the prize givers
agreed was the correct moral stand, and he did so courageously and at
the right moment.

The main character is a petty and vain writer called Norman Mailer,
a man who grows in moral stature as the book progresses. The ideas
Mailer presents are, by and large, not new. Mailer is content to report
the ideas and slogans of others in a neat package he calls Armies of the
Night: History as a Novel, the Novel as History. Mailer divides the
book into two unequal sections. The first section is a reportage of
facts as Mailer saw them. The second, while "pretending to be a history" is "some sort of collective novel."

The book opens with Mailer being talked into taking part in the 1967
march on the Pentagon by Mitchell Goodman, whose own novel, The End of It,
(the title of which Mailer could not remember) is an effective and poetic
antiwar treatise. Goodman convinces Mailer, and the latter goes to
Washington to take part in the march. On Friday, October 20, Mailer
walked to the church near the Pentagon where the march was supposed to
begin. Some of the youth leaders were eating sandwiches made of white

bread. For Mailer, white bread is a symbol of American corporate
corruption. His aversion for processed white bread is symbolic of
his execration of the corporate rule in America. Mailer illuminated
this idea in the following passage.

> The sliced loaf half-collapsed in its wax wrapper was
> the comic embodiment now of a dozen little ideas, of
> corporation-land which took the taste and crust out
> of bread and wrapped the remains in wax paper, and was,
> at the far extension of this same process, the same men-
> tality which was out in Asia . . . .[1]

The next morning everyone got ready to march. As Mailer looked
at the young people around him, dressed in startling and outlandish
costumes, he ruminated about where their radical ideas came from.
He decided in great part that they derived from the failure of the
promises made to them, the promises of the American Dream which had
been flushed away by packaged education, entertainment, and, especially, politics and commerce in which authority presented itself
as honorable while in fact it was corrupt.

> The shoddiness was buried in the package, buried some-
> where in the undiscoverable root of all those modern
> factories with the sanitized aisles and automated machines;
>
> perhaps one place the shoddiness was buried was in the
> hangovers of a working class finally alienated from any
> remote interest or attention in the process of the work
>
> itself. [pp. 103-104]

Mailer was arrested. While in jail he speculated upon the
reasons for America's involement in Vietnam. His reasons are a
summary of all the major premises written about in the newspapers
and magazines and books during and after the Vietnam war, especially
the domino theory and the threat of all out nuclear war. Mailer's
reply to these premises was that the fall of Vietnam did not threaten
American security as much as the effects of the war and its enormous
cost in money and wasted lives. For Mailer the war in Vietnam was
bad for America because it was more or less a class war and because
it had no "discernible climax." Worse, it demanded of its supporters
a suspension of the ability to reason.

To Mailer there was an even deeper reason for America's involvement
in Vietnam: he felt that the opposing poles in America of Christianity
and technology were driving America to schizophrenia,

> For the center of Christianity was a mystery, a son of
> God, and the center of the corporation was a detestation
> of mystery, a worship of technology. Nothing was more
> intrinsically opposed to technology than the bleeding
> heart of Christ. [pp. 211-212]

Book Two

The Novel as History

In this much shorter section of the book, Mailer discussed the
inaccuracy of the press, related a history of how the march had been
organized, and gave facts and statistics about the march and the marchers.

Mailer identified the protesters as being mostly of the middle class.
For him that was a paradox: one should expect the lower classes to
be the major protesters. After all, it is they who mostly do the
fighting. Yet it was the lower classes, the so-called blue-collar
workers, said, Mailer, who were the war's major supporters. The
reason was because it was the middle class that always felt most
alienated in America:

> . . . neither do they work with their hands nor wield
> great power, so it is never their lathe nor their sixty
> acres, and certainly never is it their command which is
> accepted because they are simply American . . . [p. 287]

But the psychological reasons for the protest were larger than
mere rootlessness; they centered on the need for men to assert their
masculinity: it was a way for those who did not go to war to prove
they were as brave as the soldiers who fought. Thus the protest
continued. And in that continuation Mailer saw some promise of
redemption for the sins he felt America was committing.

In Armies of the Night, Mailer repeated his ideas about what
he labels America's cannibalism, its primitive, violent, and brutal
urges, and its Christianity, its civilized, compassionate, and urbane
urges. To Mailer, America has become sick, mentally unbalanced,
schizophrenic, because those contrasting urges war within the various
social classes and often within the individual American himself. The
result is chaos—loss of perspective, lack of production, even destruction and a personal sense of longing and encasing disease.
For him, America is a spirit, perhaps even a soul, but a malign one.

He measures the effect and the progress of America's illness by
observing himself as a character, a participator, in an America
he still deeply loves, an America which is, he feels, tolerant and
sometimes even affectionate toward him, but an America which hurts
him because it is ill.

Chapter VI Notes

[1]The Armies of the Night: History as a Novel, The Novel as History

(New York, 1968), p. 77. All subsequent citations are to this edition

and are given in the text within brackets.

Chapter VII

Why Are We In Vietnam? A Novel

In an article on the modern novel, Mailer outlined the objective

he attempted in Why Are We in Vietnam?

> The realistic literature had never caught up with
>
> the rate of change in American life, indeed, it had
>
> fallen further and further behind, and the novel gave
>
> up any desire to be a creation equal to the phenomenon
>
> of the country itself; it settled for being a meta-
>
> phor which is to say that each separate author made a
>
> separate peace. He would no longer try to capture
>
> America, he would merely try to give life to some
>
> microcosm in American life, some metaphor—in the sense
>
> that a drop of water is for some a metaphor of the beast.[1]

In the case of Why Are We in Vietnam? an eighteen-year-old soldier on

his way to Vietnam, D.J. Jethroe, and the world D.J. inhabits, become

a microcosm of America, presented in dream-like proportions. Realism

and ratiocenation are not present in the novel.

D.J. is the hero and narrator. He tells about a hunting trip on

which he went to the Brooks Range in Alaska when he was sixteen, a

hunting trip which has affected D. J.'s perceptions enormously. In

his own metaphor, D. J. is "Disk Jock to America . . . ." He broad-

casts his prophecies in the language of "Hip," a language much akin

to Black American English. Even his subheadings flow within his

metaphorical stream of narrative. There are chapters called "Chap"
in parody of the big business shorthand which added such words as
"comp" and "A-OK" to our language. There are interchapters called
"intro beeps" in parody of the hip-illusion world of radio.

Like many of Mailer's characters, D.J. is on a quest for identity.
". . . What if I'm not the white George Hamilton rich son of Dallas,
Texas [he asks], and Hallelujah ass but am instead black . . . ." It
is a question he will ask many times throughout the book. He confuses
his source of "hip," his fantasy self in Harlem, with his own "hip."

From what can be gathered, he is the son of David Rutherford,
"Rusty," Jethroe, a rich Texas plastics firm executive, and Alice
Hallie Jethroe. Like Stephen Rojack of An American Dream, D.J. sees
the confusion of the world coming about because "God has always wanted
more from man than man has wished to give him." As the leaves of the
book unfold, he begins to analyze why America became involved in Vietnam.
He gives seven basic reasons. The first is that the American male's
sexual habits are too closely linked to his quest for violence. A
second reason is because the psychological or corporational jargon
America uses impedes communication. D.J. parodies this language
throughout the book.

In an imaginary conversation by his mother, D.J. describes America's
obsession with cleanliness, the third cause of America's being in
Vietnam. The effects of this obsession can be seen in the metaphors
of any American newspaper of the Vietnam era. The enemy is described
as being "dirty." The Americans are always described as "cleaning
out" an enemy stronghold.

Mailer's fourth reason for America's involement in Vietnam is that it is a nation not of "flowers," but of "weeds," whose struggle is neither for beauty nor for light, but frankly for supremacy over other weeds. And this supremacy involves the crowding out and choking off of everything but themselves in order to make ever increasing room for their own never ceasing expansion.

Reason number five is the increasing dehumanization of life, the replacing of man by machines. D.J. carries this idea in his metaphors. For example, he describes DNA and RNA as being a tape recorder within his brain and cells, subject to future tapping by men, or by God Himself. This dehumanization of life Mailer identifies with his idea that ". . . we are all after all agents of Satan and the Lord. . . ." As it does to Rojack, this realization leaves D.J. "up tight with the concept of dread." The only way to rid oneself of dread, Mailer explained in An American Dream, is to risk one's life. Often one must do so deliberately, says Mailer. That is why Americans are so fascinated with hunting, with weapons (for example, pages 77-84 of the novel are devoted to the naming of rifles), and with war. But the complex of dread, sexuality, and risk cannot always be resolved by the individual in hunting or in war because of the rather limited accessibility of such forms of release and their failure as virtual violence. It is relieved within the power structure of business and the corporate "team."

The corporate team is a variation of the Cummings' military structure that Mailer wrote about in The Naked and the Dead. Both hold the view that power must be achieved no matter what the social

cost. For example, that the largest selling product of the company
D.J.'s father works for is a cigarette filter the company knows
causes cancer of the lip is not important. What is important to
Rusty is that the filter's sales have enabled him to climb the corporate power ladder. Rusty Jethroe is also a booster and a joiner.
But all the organizations he belongs to diffuse his energies. The
list of clubs and organizations, often contradictory, to which Rusty
belongs covers two pages. It is no wonder then that D.J. describes
his father as having the same feelings consummating a business affair
as he does consummating a sexual affair.

Mailer also sees America's obsession with sex as another problem
which led to Vietnam. In an interview with a European correspondant,
Mailer said,

> One way or another you Europeans always manage to keep
> your minds busy, so you can afford the luxury of abandoning
> yourself to sex without being obsessed by it. We can't.
> Without roots, having few thoughts, we use sex to fill our
> lives.[2]

Business is a part of that search for love which Mailer defined as
"orgasm more apocalyptic than the one before." Occurring on the individual level it is the same confrontation of power that McLeod describes in Barbary Shore as being between the powers of social and
monopoly capitalism. The ultimate result, says Mailer, is violent
release on the social level. This release is war.

But on the personal level such release may be had on a hunting
trip. The hunting trip may also be a way to impress those higher up
on the corporate fear ladder. Because America is a nation of exhibitionists

says Mailer, be it flashier clothes, larger hunting trophies, or more
fawning, grateful nations, Rusty knows that if he can come home with a
big bear his higher-ups will promote him. Naturally, the method of
achieving that trophy is of no importance. The only important thing
is the results it brings, namely more personal power. As such, Rusty
is symbolic of American leadership, just as General Cummings was in
The Naked and the Dead.

But Rusty's son D.J. is going on the hunting trip for another
reason. In Cannibals and Christians, Mailer wrote that to be truly
intimate with God, one must share what Mailer calls the "Divine terror."

> If intimacy with God is not merely a communion of love
> but a sharing of the Divine terror, then the beauty of
> any miracle delivered by God is always accompanied by
> a fear proportionate to the beauty. Because a miracle
> is not merely a breach in the laws of nature, but a
> revelation of the nature of the God behind nature. If
> one cannot undergo the fear, one does not deserve the
> revelation.[3]

Therefore, D.J., who wants to capture dread and become "hip," must,
like Rojack in An American Dream, face dread in order to overcome it.
He chooses to do so deliberately by going with his father to Alaska in
order to kill a bear. But once on the trip, he begins to realize just
how close is the parallel between the violence of killing animals on a
hunt and the violence of killing men in war, be it hot, cold, or class.
The parallel becomes clear to him when his father, the guide, and his
father's assistants describe the killing of grizzly bear in terms of

military lore.

D.J. learns more about the real world when he and Rusty take off
to look for bear alone and on foot. He discovers another side of his
father, of the corporate man, which is never allowed public show.
Rusty has a true sensitivity for flowers, and for nature, which he
can display only when alone with his son or with his wife, or with
his guide, Big Luke. He reveals to D.J. that at age sixteen, "I used
to be a walking compendium of Texas wildflowers." But such wealth and
delight in nature has been replaced by pleasure in financial gain. And
that is a sixth reason why America became involved in Vietnam: the en-
joyment of sensitivity to nature has been buried by a desire for land
in its natural state under the name of "real estate," the acquisition
of lands for pragmatic purposes. Rusty describes this fault of America
in metaphorical terms when he tells D.J.

> "I think it's a secret crime that America, which is the
> greatest nation ever lived . . . is nontheless represented,
> indeed, even symbolized by an eagle, the most miserable of
> the scavengers, worse than crow." [4]

Soon D.J. himself becomes more sensitive to the lessons one can
learn from nature, the messages it sends. As he becomes more attuned
to nature, his sense of smell becomes extrasensory. Like Rojack, in
An American Dream, he begins to smell not simply odors, but psychic
states as well. For example, when he and Rusty see a grizzly bear,
he says, "And D.J. breathes death, first time in his life . . ." Soon

he equates the bear with dread, the thing that he must overcome to
become "hip." For him it becomes Mr. D. Yet what makes D.J. go
on to face the bear, especially at first, is nothing more than peer
group pressure. He is afraid his friend Tex will think badly of him.

Unlike Steven Rojack, D.J. chooses defeat. It is not clear
whether he does so out of fear or compassion, but either way he fails
to achieve that "cruelty to be a man" that so many of Mailer's protagonists strive for, because D.J. cannot kill the bear that he and
his father had wounded. He discovers that he has too much compassion
for it.

He then describes himself as ". . . marooned on the balmy tropical
island of Anal Referent Metaphor," in which "excrement is defeat." As
Mailer wrote in Cannibals and Christians, excrement is also symbolic
of something larger:

Vision is the mind of God; soul His body; and Spirit is
what He has left behind. Literally. It is His excrement.[5]

But when the bear dies from the wounds inflicted earlier by D.J. and his
father, they go back to camp and Rusty claims full credit for the kill.
D.J. then realizes that he must reject the corporate mode of morality
which his father represents and go back out with his friend Tex and
try to achieve autonomous power. What he discovers is an awareness
of the psychic forces that Rojack found working in the universe. He
learns of the individual's transmission of electromagnetic waves during
sleep. These waves flow throughout the continent,Mailer claims, and
affect human attitudes and animal behavior. In Mailer's cosmology,
any interruption of the flow of the magnetic field created by the flow

of psychic forces causes depression in man and a sense of annoyance.
Mailer suggests that this depression is symptomatic of the fact that
we are out of touch with the universe, with God. The philosophers of
the Middle Ages were right: harmony is God's voice in nature, in art,
and in us. D.J. begins to perceive these things when he learns that
"all the messages of North America go up to the Brooks Range." It is
from there that the messages are transmitted to either God or the devil,
principally, Mailer conjectures, because of the parabolic shape of the
range, and because of the superconductivity resulting from the extreme
cold.

Thus, as all of Mailer's major protagonists do, D.J. has now gotten
himself into a position where he can begin to struggle to advance his
personal power and thereby to advance the power of God. As in The Naked
and the Dead, Mailer symbolizes D.J.'s struggle for personal power in
his battle to climb a mountain.

With D.J. goes Tex, his best friend. D.J. and Tex begin in a
spirit of comradship, trading friendly insults, being careful not to
let their true emotions show. When it gets dark, they witness the
aurora borealis and D.J. thinks that he feels the presence of God.
For him God is a beast-like presence that says to him "Go and kill—
fulfill my will, go and kill . . ." D.J. confuses God with the devil
and so chooses evil, which is defeat and the opposite of creation. He
nearly chooses non-creation on a more immediate level: homosexuality,
the corporate latent homosexuality of his father, the post war corporate man, whose very "manliness" is, like General Cumming's "manliness

manifested in a concern only for impressing other men. This is the
seventh reason why America became involved in Vietnam. In confusing
the devil of destruction with God of creation, America has confused
the essentially homosexual desire of men to impress other men with
their "masculinity" by pursuing destructive pseudoheterosexual pastimes
such as hunting or war with the true heterosexual, or creative pastime
which is the search for love.

D.J. knows all this and yet like many of Mailer's heroes from Red
Valsen to Steven Rojack, he is unable to act. The most that he can do
is to revert to ritual, as did Rojack. However, in D.J.'s case, it is
the primitive Indian ritual of blood brotherhood that he performs with
Tex. They cut their fingers and suck the blood. But it is a latent
homosexual brotherhood based upon predatory impulses and death, and
leading to Vietnam. This idea is nowhere better illustrated than in
D.J.'s admission that he and Tex often fornicate with the same Texas
matrons, and that both share a kind of necrophiliac voyeurism in their
fascination with the corpses of Tex's father's funeral home, and that,
indeed, D.J. has volunteered for the Army and for Vietnam only because
Tex did.

His friend Tex is going to Vietnam to "prove his masculinity,"
and so to enter into the corporate mainstream. But D.J. is on his
way because he is being controlled by others. He has no choice because he has no real will of his own. Very much like Major Dalleson
in The Naked and the Dead, D.J. can merely become enthusiastic about
the ritual of living within the power structure the way it is, and
hope that in Vietnam he will get the opportunity to face real dread

and so have the chance to become autonomous. He has had an opportunity
to receive and to send messages of God, but too much American civilization
has deadened his synapses. That is why D.J. does not understand the
messages that are coming to him. Like most modern men he is out of
touch with his own psyche and even with his own physical self. So he
is a soldier on the way to Vietnam as the novel ends. "Vietnam," he
says, "hot damn." One cannot help notice the parallel between the ending of this novel and the ending of The Naked and the Dead.

In commenting upon the title of the book, James Toback has said,
"In an ultimate sense Mailer is claiming not only relation to America
but identity with her."[6] Mailer has come full circle in his fiction.
He began with a realistic novel that explored the American power structure
In Why Are We in Vietnam? he explores through the use of metaphor the
reasons for the war in Vietnam. But in all of these novels he has been
concerned with power and how it really works.

Chapter VII

Notes

[1] Norman Mailer, "Modes and Mutations: A Comment on the American Novel," *Commentary*, XLI (March, 1966), 39.

[2] Oricana Fallaci, "Interview with Norman Mailer," *Writer's Digest*, XLIX (December, 1969), 81.

[3] *Cannibals and Christians*, p. 377.

[4] *Why Are We in Vietnam? A Novel* (New York, 1967), pp. 132-133. All subsequent citations are to this edition and are given in the text within brackets.

[5] *Cannibals and Christians*, p. 365.

[6] James Toback, "Norman Mailer Today," *Commentary*, XLIV (October, 1967), 74.

Chapter VIII

Marilyn

Marilyn is a new species, or subspecies. It is part biography,
part fiction. In it, Mailer claims to bring his "novelist's insight"
to explore the aura and the metaphor of Marilyn Monroe, the "sweet
angel of sex." While for many readers this phrase, "sweet angel of
sex," may seem a bit paradoxical, Mailer seems to be trying to imply
by it the definitive truth in his very personal theological system
in which the devil is God-in-banishment, and physical sex God's Ultimate Truth. In Marilyn Mailer claims once again that in the post
World War II world fact is fiction and fiction is fact. He seems to
be claiming that too often the dream is perceived as reality, and
reality the dream created by mass media. In Marilyn the concepts
originally worked out in An American Dream and Why Are We in Vietnam?
A Novel are tested against the mythic-real heroine and her world.
Mailer believes that Marilyn in some ways helped to define that decade
of the Kennedys and Martin Luther King. He implies that metaphorically
at least, physically and factually at most, her death gave birth and
nourishment to the even more bewildering age of Richard Nixon's power.
In other words, Mailer claims that Marilyn was some sort of archetype
in the American Dream.

Mailer insists that even more than most lives, Marilyn's cannot
be understood by the mere facts. Perhaps that is why he never bothered
to check too carefully the facts he presented in Marilyn. Instead,

he suggests that those who want a factual biography should consult
those from which he most liberally borrowed. As for him, he will
present a "literary hypothesis of a possible Marilyn Monroe, one who
might actually have lived and fit most of the facts available."

> Set a thief to catch a thief, and put an artist on an
> artist. Could the solution be nothing less vainglorious
> than a novel of Marilyn Monroe? Written in the form of
> biography? Since it would hardly be more than a long
> biographical article--nontheless, a species of novel
> ready to play by the rules of biography.[1]

But therein lies the problem. Mailer does not really present facts,
but what he calls "factoids." He uses this term to label the shoddy
offspring of his unequal mating of fact and fiction. The more usual
term in English for them is "half-truths." Because the book relies
on "factoids," it is robbed of both the process by which truth is
fashioned out of fiction and the empirical proof with which a post-
eriori theorums are built.

As if factoids weren't enough, Marilyn has stylistic faults as well.
In his enthusiasm for the subject, Mailer over-writes, and thus often
painfully overstates his case, unintentionally courting both caricature
and burlesque with ironic deliberation. The following quote will
illustrate:

> Yet during the filming of Let's Make Love she was to write
> in her dressing room notebook, "what am I afraid of? Why
> am I so afraid? . . . I am afraid and I should not be and
> I must not be." It is in fear and trembling that she writes.

> In dread. Nothing less than some intimation of the death
>
> of her soul may be in her fear. But then is it not hope-
>
> less to comprehend her without some concept of a soul?
>
> One might literally have to invent the idea of a soul
>
> in order to approach her "What am I afraid of?" [p. 17]

Here Mailer tries to claim metaphysical speculations worthy of a Kierkegaard or a Nietzche for what is no more than a rather prosaic and thoroughly adolescent statement.

There are many trite or overworked phrases and sentiments such as the following:

> In a career like Monroe's where no one can be certain
>
> whether she was playing an old role, experimenting with
>
> a new one, or even being nothing less than the true self
>
> (which she spent her life trying to discover) . . . . [p. 18]

The extreme overuse of exclamation points and dashes demonstrate all too well that for the first time in his career Norman Mailer has written a book with too much zeal and too little care, caution, craft, or time. There is no excuse for such statements as "no, the New York Daily News won't be on her side no more."

Mailer constantly poses subjunctive questions but denies the sub-junctive mood. For example, he writes, "if she was bound to be some-what unstable considering the concentrated insanity of her inheritance. This avoidance of the subjunctive mood makes it seem as if Mailer were trading present speculation for past certainties, whether truly certain or not. Perhaps the stylistic problems of the book have deep telling implications all their own: in none of the characters of the book,

including Marilyn herself, has Mailer created a novelist's universality
or a biographer's accuracy.

Further, since Mailer labels Marilyn a species of biographical
novel, he is forced back to the techniques of biographical determinism
of The Naked and the Dead and the prewar realist novelists who needed
to construct whole histories of their subjects and to follow their
development. With Marilyn, Mailer must go back to the determined in-
securities, real or imagined, of an illegitimate birth, a near strangulation
in the cradle, and a family history of insanity. We are reminded of the
cancer killed corpse who is America at the end of An American Dream.
Mailer, who professes belief in a kind of Karma, says of Marilyn and
of others who are exceptional that her life was unhappy because of the
debt she owed existence for an earlier life lived without courage or
success.

In the story of Marilyn's early life, especially in the family
insanity and her near suffocation or smothering as a child, and her
survival, Mailer sees the American "pride of the weed that knows it
is the true flower of the garden" that D.J. spoke about in Why Are We
in Vietnam? as well as the will-to-destruction which caused the mental
breakdown of Sergius in The Deer Park. Mailer speculates that her attempt to keep from revealing her real identity both from herself and
from others is a metaphorical echo of the larger social problem of
"how much the Silent Majority lives in dread of the danger which lies
beneath appearances," and of the impossibility "for people who live in
institutions not to tell lies, since an institution works best if none
of the inmates tells the truth." Likewise, Mailer, who has a great

fondness for orphans, psychic and otherwise, sees in Marilyn's orphanage days the incipience of her destructive narcissism and a microcosm of America's will-to-destruction. Mailer continues the connection by attaching great importance to Marilyn's relation with a Christian Scientist by the name of Ana Lower. Yet there is more: It will be recalled that Mailer believes that everyone, and the great more than the average, send messages upon which the battle between God and the devil depends. Thus, every shock and boredom of those early years builds potential energies within Marilyn not simply for her own personal future but for the future of God-in-banishment. Her failure, Mailer speculates, is God's failure. And the apocalypse becomes that much more determined. Hence her death brings Richard Nixon to power in America, and God knows, or rather doesn't know, Who into power in the universe.

In *An American Dream* there is a description of an act of sodomy between the hero, Steven Rojack, and Ruta, the maid; other acts of sodomy are suggested in *Why Are We in Vietnam?* and elsewhere in Mailer's fiction. In all of these episodes, Mailer makes it clear that, in his personal theology, the anus represents the forces of evil, sterility, and death. What Mailer implies, then, in his description of Marilyn's undulating hips, is her end:

> "Take me from behind, I'm yours," say her undulating
> hips. A blond with an anal bent is looking for the
> towers of power. [p. 79]

Mailer calls her contract with the motion picture studio "Faustian," and implies that much of her life has been lived under contract to the

Devil-in-power, whom most people call God. Perhaps because of this
contract it is impossible for Marilyn to establish her true identity.
She further complicates this problem by choosing to mask what identity
she has, not only by inventing "factoids," but by performing the great
American melting-pot ritual: she has plastic surgery on her nose and
chin. Norma Jean hides her true self as she searches for it. Perhaps it is for this reason that Mailer identifies Marilyn as a metaphor of America. The more she searches, the more she hides. It is
no wonder her search leads inevitably to a bottle of barbituates.
She moves faster toward death than most people, pushed by her drive
toward some new or ultimate identity. Thus, Mailer sees in her refusal to marry the rich movie producer Johnny Hyde and so become for-
ever financially independant, such a dichotomous struggle for identity.
As his widow she would have been merely "Mrs. Hyde." She would not
have her own identity, and "some," says Mailer, "will give up love or
security before they dare to lose the comfort of identity."

Ironically, however, the more she loses her sense of personal
identity and power, the more she gains public identity and power until
she becomes that highest form of American celebrity, a "household word."
But the price has been the loss of any semblance of a private life and
any genuine personal emotions. That she takes drugs to avoid having
any real emotions is, for Mailer, symbolic of America's refusal to
engage the supernatural, to face dread.

A number of years ago Mailer had written in Advertisements for
Myself that the post World War II generation of writers had stopped
trying to produce the Great American Novel. Instead they substituted
the novel of metaphor, allowing "the hair of the beast to stand for
the beast itself." In some ways, Mailer claims that Marilyn is such

a metaphorical novel. Out of the life of Marilyn Monroe, Mailer
tried to create a metaphor for that post war generation of which
he found himself a part, with all the attending myths that generation
believed in, running the gamut from the will-to-power of the Kennedy
clan to the masculinity myth of sex-without-involvement. In describing
Marilyn's real relationship with Joe DiMaggio, for example, and her
probably metaphorical relationship with Bobby Kennedy, Mailer explores
(as he does in his other works of fiction) what he considers the
potential sources of power and autonomy. But Marilyn, being neither
quite biography or novel, suffers because facts are distorted into
"factoids," and the integrity of the artist is lost.

Chapter VIII Notes

[1]Marilyn (New York, 1973), p.20. All subsequent citations are to this
edition and are given in the text within brackets.

A BIOGRAPHICAL NOTE

BIBLIOGRAPHY,

BIOGRAPHY AND AUTOBIOGRAPHY :   With his first

success in 1948, Norman Mailer received a short biographical
entry in Current Biography, New York, H.W. Wilson, 1948, pp.
408-410. Some years later much of the same material was repeated and updated in Twentieth Century Authors, First Sup-
lement, 1955, ed. Stanley J. Kunitz (New York, 1955),pp. 628-
629. The first biography with any pretense toward full bibliography was compiled in 1957 by Robin Nelson Downes (A
Bio-Bibliography of Norman Mailer). It is available from
Florida State University, but only on microcard. As might
be expected from the title, there is more bib than bio in
this graphy. Of more interest to anyone seeking to learn
about Mailer himself is Barry H. Leeds' The Structured Vision
of Norman Mailer, New York, New York University Press, 1970.
Leeds focuses on Mailer's career and how Mailer's personal
image has influenced and clouded opinions about his writing.
In this respect, Robert F. Lucid's editing of Norman Mailer:
The Man and His Works, 1971, is also quite lucid.

There are a number of good interviews with Mailer.
Especially interesting for various reasons are Eve Auchencloss
and Nancy Lynch's interview for Mademoiselle (Feb. 1961), 76-
77; 160-163, and Harry Breit's "A Talk with Norman Mailer,"
Times Book Review LVI (June 3, 1951),20. The latter was reprinted
in The Writer Observed, 1956, pp. 199-201. The best and most
helpful interviews, however, are Oriana Fallaci's in Writer's
Digest, 1967, Steven Marcus' in Paris Review (Winter-Spring
1964), reprinted in Paris Review Interviews, 3rd
Series, 1967, pp.251-278. Probably the most influential
interview, and the one Mailer himself is most fond of, is
Richard G. Stern, "Hip, Hell, and the Navigator: An Interview
With Norman Mailer," Western Review, XXIII (1959), 101-109.

CRITICAL Of the few full-length treatments of Norman
BOOKS: Mailer's works, probably the best was Richard
      Poirier's Norman Mailer, 1972. Donald Kaufmann's
Norman Mailer: The Countdown(The First Twenty Years), 1969, is
also quite good, despite its rather gimmicky format. Kaufmann's
book is a reworking of his doctoral dissertation on Mailer,
which he wrote under the direction of Edmund Skellings, a
personal friend and frequent interviewer of Mailer. Barry
Leeds' The Structured Vision of Norman Mailer, 1969, is also

well worthwhile. A much shorter study, really a monograph,
Richard Foster's "Norman Mailer," the 73rd number of the
University of Minnesota's Publications on American Writers,
casts a colder eye on Mailer's literary output before 1968,
when the monograph first appeared. Also worthy of perusal
are the sections on Mailer in Howard M. Harper Jr!'s Desperate
Faith: A Study of Salinger, Mailer, Baldwin, and Updike, 1967.

CRITICAL   When Mailer began calling himself an
ARTICLES: existentialist, many critics listened to
                him. Of the dozen or so articles which
deal with Mailer's existentialist theme, the best are Bruce
M. Cook,"Norman Mailer, The Temptation to Power," Renaissance
XIV (Summer 1962); George Alfred Schrader, "Norman Mailer
and the Despair of Defiance, Yale Review LI (1961); Alfred
Kazin, "Imagination and the Age," Reporter XXXIV (May 5, 1966);
and Samuel Hux, "Mailer's Dream of Violence," Minnesota
Review," VIII (1968).

Among the more general articles the best and most balanced
are Ihab Hassan,"The Way Down and Out," Virginia Quarterly
Review, XXXIX (Winter 1963), 81-93, and David Hesla, "The
Two Roles of Norman Mailer." This essay is most readily
available in Adversity and Grace: Studies in Recent American

Literature, edited by Nathan A. Scott, Jr. *Adversity and Grace* is a fine edition, solidly edited.

Mailer's moral code is the subject of Diana Trilling's "Norman Mailer," *Encounter* XIX (November 1962). It was reprinted as "The Radical Moralism of Norman Mailer " in *The Creative Present*, edited by Nora Balakain and Charles Simmons, 1963. Perhaps the single best article dealing with Mailer's early work is Norman Podhoretz, "Norman Mailer: The Embattled Vision," *Partisan Review*, XXVI (Summer 1959). If back issues of *Partisan Review* are not available to you, don't despair. The article was reprinted as the introduction to *Barbary Shore*, again in *Recent American Fiction: Some Critical Views*, edited by Joseph J. Waldmur, and still again in *Doings and Undoings: The Fifties and After in American Writing*.

WORKS BY MAILER

Mailer, Norman. Advertisements For Myself. New York, 1959.

_____ "Advertisements for Myself on the Way Out." Partisan
Review XXV (1958), 519-540.

_____ An American Dream (Published Serially) Esquire LXI
(January, 1964), 77-81; (February) 107; (March) 89-92;
(April) 97-100; (May) 124-127; (June) 114-116; (July)
41-42; (August) 41-43.

_____ The Armies of the Night. New York, 1968.

_____ Barbary Shore, New York, 1951.

_____ "Big Bite," Esquire LVIII (November, 1962), 134;
(December), 168; LVIX (January, 1963), 65.

_____ Cannibals and Christians. New York, 1966.

_____ "Cities Higher Than Mountains," New York Times
Magazine (January 31, 1965), 16-18.

———— "Classes," <u>New</u> <u>Statesman</u> LXV (February 8, 1963) 207.

———— <u>Deaths</u> <u>for</u> <u>the</u> <u>Ladies</u> <u>and</u> <u>Other</u> <u>Disasters</u>. New York 1962.

———— <u>The</u> <u>Deer</u> <u>Park</u>. New York, 1955.

———— <u>The</u> <u>Deer</u> <u>Park</u>, <u>A</u> <u>Play</u>. New York, 1967.

———— "Eternities" <u>New</u> <u>Yorker</u> XXXVII (November 11, 1961) 200.

———— <u>Existential</u> <u>Errands</u>. Boston, 1972.

———— "An Evening With Jackie Kennedy." <u>Esquire</u> LVIII (July 1962) 56-61.

———— "Fire on the Moon." <u>Life</u> LXVII (August 29, 1969) 24-42.

———— "The First Day's Interview." <u>Paris</u> <u>Review</u> XXVI (Summer-Fall, 1961), 140-153.

———— "In the Red Light: A History of the Republican Convention in 1964," <u>Esquire</u> LXII (November, 1964), 83-89.

———— "Last Night," <u>Esquire</u> LX (December 1963), 151.

————— Maidstone, a Mystery. New York. 1971.

——— Marilyn. New York. 1973.

——— Miami and the Seige of Chicago; An Informal History of the Republican and Democratic Conventions of 1968, New York, 1968.

————— "The Mind of an Outlaw," Esquire LI (May 1959), 87-90, 92, 94.

————— "Modes and Mutations: Comment on the Modern American Novel," Commentary VII (March 1966) 37-40.

————— The Naked and the Dead. New York, 1948.

————— "Norman Mailer Versus Nine Writers," Esquire LX (1963), 63-69,105.

————— "Playboy Interview: Norman Mailer." Playboy XV (January, 1968), 69-84.

————— Of a Fire on the Moon. Boston, 1970.

————— The Presidential Papers. New York, 1963.

————— The Prisoner of Sex. Boston, 1971.

—————— "Quick and Expansive Comments on the Talent in the Room," Big Table III (1959), 88-100.

—————— "Reply to Gore Vidal," Nation CXC (January 30, 1960), inside cover.

—————— "Reply to 'Mystique De la Merde,' " Time LXVIII (October 1, 1956), 94.

—————— "Responses and Reactions; Excerpts from The Presidential Papers." Commentary XXXIV (December, 1962) 504-506; XXXV (April, 1963) 146-148; (June, 1963) 335-337; (August, 1963) 517-518; XXXVI (October, 1963) 320-321.

—————— "Some Children of the Goddess," Contemporary American Novelists ed. Henry Thornton Moore. Carbondale, Illinois, 1964.

—————— "Some Dirt in the Talk: a Candid History of an Existential Movie Called Wild 90." Esquire LXVIII (December, 1961) 190-195.

—————— "10,000 Words a Minute," Esquire LIX (February,

COSTERUS. Essays in English and American Language and Literature.

Volume 1. Amsterdam 1972. 240 p. Hfl. 40.—
GARLAND CANNON: Sir William Jones's Translation-Interpretation of Sanskrit Literature. SARAH DYCK: The Presence of that Shape: Shelley's *Prometheus Unbound*. MARJORIE ELDER: Hawthorne's *The Marble Faun:* A Gothic Structure. JAMES L. GOLDEN: Adam Smith as a Rhetorical Theorist and Literary Critic. JACK GOODSTEIN: Poetry, Religion and Fact: Matthew Arnold. JAY L. HALIO: Anxiety in *Othello.* JOHN ILLO: Miracle in Milton's Early Verse. F. SAMUEL JANZOW: De Quincey's "Danish Origin of the Lake Country Dialect" Republished. MARTIN L. KORNBLUTH: The Degeneration of Classical Friendship in Elizabethan Drama. VIRGINIA MOSELY: The "Dangerous" Paradox in Joyce's "Eveline". JOHN NIST: Linguistics and the Esthetics of English. SCOTT B. RICE: Smollett's *Travels* and the Genre of Grand Tour Literature. LISBETH J. SACHS and BERNARD H. STERN: The Little Preoedipal Boy in Papa Hemingway and How He Created His Artistry.

Volume 2. Amsterdam 1972. 236 p. Hfl. 40.—
RALPH BEHRENS: Mérimée, Hemingway, and the Bulls. JEANNINE BOHL-MEYER: Mythology in Sackville's "Induction" and "Complaint". HAROLD A. BRACK: Needed — a new language for communicating religion. LEONARD FEINBERG: Satire and Humor: In the Orient and in the West. B. GRANGER: The Whim-Whamsical Bachelors in Salmagundi. W. M. FORCE: The What Story? or Who's Who at the Zoo? W. N. KNIGHT: To Enter lists with God. Transformation of Spencerian Chivalric Tradition in Paradise Regained. MARY D. KRAMER: The Roman Catholic Cleric on the Jacobean Stage. BURTON R. POLLIN: The Temperance Movement and Its Friends Look at Poe. SAMUEL J. ROGAL: Two Translations of the Iliad, Book I: Pope and Tickell. J. L. STYAN: The Delicate Balance: Audience Ambivalence in the Comedy of Shakespeare and Chekhov. CLAUDE W. SUMERLIN: Christopher Smart's A Song to David: its influence on Robert Browning. B.W. TEDFORD: A Recipe for Satire and Civilization. H. H. WATTS: Othello and the Issue of Multiplicity. GUY R. WOODALL: Nationalism in the Philadelphia National Gazette and Literary Register: 1820–1836.

Volume 3. Amsterdam 1972. 236 p. Hfl. 40.—
RAYMOND BENOIT: In Dear Detail by Ideal Light: "Ode on a Grecian Urn". E. F. CALLAHAN: Lyric Origins of the Unity of 1 Henry IV. FRASER DREW: John Masefield and Juan Manuel de Rosas. LAURENCE GONZALEZ: Persona Bob: seer and fool. A. HIRT: A Question of Excess: Neo-Classical Adaptations of Greek Tragedy. EDWIN HONIG: Examples of

Poetic Diction in Ben Jonson. ELSIE LEACH: T. S. Eliot and the School of Donne. SEYMOUR REITER: The Structure of 'Waiting for Godot'. DANIEL E. VAN TASSEL: The Search for Manhood in D. H. Lawrence's 'Sons and Lovers'. MARVIN ROSENBERG: Poetry of the Theatre. GUY R. WOOD-ALL: James Russell Lowell's "Works of Jeremy Taylor, D.D.'

Volume 4. Amsterdam 1972. 233 p. Hfl. 40.—
BOGDDY ARIAS: Sailor's Reveries. R. H. BOWERS: Marlowe's 'Dr. Faustus', Tirso's 'El Condenado por Desconfiado', and the Secret Cause. HOWARD O. BROGAN: Satirist Burns and Lord Byron. WELLER EMBLER: Simone Weil and T. S. Eliot. E. ANTHONY JAMES: Defoe's Autobiographical Apologia: Rhetorical Slanting in 'An Appeal to Honour and Justice'. MARY D. KRAMER: The American Wild West Show and "Buffalo Bill" Cody. IRVING MASSEY: Shelley's "Dirge for the Year": The Relation of the Holograph to the First Edition. L. J. MORRISSEY: English Street Theatre: 1655—1708. M. PATRICK: Browning's Dramatic Techniques and 'The Ring and the Book': A Study in Mechanic and Organic Unity. VINCENT F. PETRONELLA: Shakespeare's 'Henry V' and the Second Tetralogy: Meditation as Drama. NASEEB SHAHEEN: Deriving Adjectives from Nouns. TED R. SPIVEY: The Apocalyptic Symbolism of W. B. Yeats and T. S. Eliot. EDWARD STONE: The Other Sermon in 'Moby—Dick'. M. G. WILLIAMS: 'In Memoriam': A Broad Church Poem.

Volume 5. Amsterdam 1972. 236 p. Hfl. 40.—
PETER G. BEIDLER: Chaucer's Merchant and the Tale of January. ROBERT A. BRYAN: Poets, Poetry, and Mercury in Spenser's Prosopopia: Mother Hubberd's Tale. EDWARD M. HOLMES: Requiem For A Scarlet Nun. E. ANTHONY JAMES: Defoe's Narrative Artistry: Naming and Describing in Robinson Crusoe. MICHAEL J. KELLY: Coleridge's "Picture, or The Lover's Resolution": its Relationship to "Dejection" and its Sources in the Notebooks. EDWARD MARGOLIES: The Playwright and his Critics. MURRAY F. MARKLAND: The Task Set by Valor. RAYMOND S. NELSON: Back to Methuselah: Shaw's Modern Bible. THOMAS W. ROSS: Maimed Rites in Much Ado About Nothing. WILLIAM B. TOOLE: The Metaphor of Alchemy in Julius Caesar. PAUL WEST: Carlyle's Bravura Prophetics. GLENA D. WOOD: The Tragi-Comic Dimensions of Lear's Fool. H. ALAN WYCHERLEY: "Americana": The Mencken — Lorimer Feud.

Volume 6. Amsterdam 1972. 235 p. Hfl. 40.—
GEORG W. BOSWELL: Superstition and Belief in Faulkner. ALBERT COOK: Blake's Milton. MARSHA KINDER: The Improved Author's Farce: An Analysis of the 1734 Revisions. ABE LAUFE: What Makes Drama Run? (Introduction to Anatomy of a Hit). RICHARD L. LOUGHLIN: Laugh and Grow Wise with Oliver Goldsmith. EDWARD MARGOLIES: The American Detective Thriller & The Idea of Society. RAYMOND S. NELSON: Shaw's Heaven, Hell, and Redemption. HAROLD OREL: Is Patrick White's Voss the Real Leichhardt of Australia? LOUIS B. SALOMON: A Walk With Emerson On The Dark Side. H. GRANT SAMPSON: Structure in the Poetry of Thoreau. JAMES H. SIMS, Some Biblical Light on Shakespeare's Hamlet.

ROBERT F. WILLSON, Jr.: Lear's Auction. JAMES N. WISE: Emerson's "Experience" and "Sons and Lovers". JAMES D. YOUNG: Aims in Reader's Theatre.

Volume 7. Amsterdam 1973. 235 p. Hfl. 40.–
HANEY H. BELL Jr.: Sam Fathers and Ike McCaslin and the World in Which Ike Matures. SAMUEL IRVING BELLMAN: The Apocalypse in Literature. HALDEEN BRADDY: England and English before Alfred. DAVID R. CLARK: Robert Frost: "The Thatch" and "Directive". RALPH MAUD: Robert Crowley, Puritan Satirist. KATHARINE M. MORSBERGER: Hawthorne's "Borderland": The Locale of the Romance. ROBERT E. MORSBERGER: The Conspiracy of the Third International. "What is the metre of the dictionary? " – Dylan Thomas. RAYMOND PRESTON: Dr. Johnson and Aristotle. JOHN J. SEYDOW: The Sound of Passing Music: John Neal's Battle for American Literary Independence. JAMES H. SIMS: Enter Satan as Esau, Alone; Exit Satan as Belshazzar: *Paradise Lost,* BOOK (IV). MICHAEL WEST, Dryden and the Disintegration of Renaissance Heroic Ideals. RENATE C. WOLFF: Pamela as Myth and Dream.

Volume 8. Amsterdam 1973. 231 p. Hfl. 40.–
SAMUEL I. BELLMAN: Sleep, Pride, and Fantasy: Birth Traumas and Socio-Biologic Adaptation in the American-Jewish Novel. PETER BUITEN-HUIS: A Corresponding Fabric: The Urban World of Saul Bellow. DAVID R. CLARK: An Excursus upon the Criticism of Robert Frost's "Directive". FRANCIS GILLEN: Tennyson and the Human Norm: A Study of Hubris and Human Commitment in Three Poems by Tennyson. ROBERT R. HARSON: H. G. Wells: The Mordet Island Episode. JULIE B. KLEIN: The Art of Apology: "An Epistle to Dr. Arbuthnot" and "Verses on the Death of Dr. Swift". ROBERT E. MORSBERGER: The Movie Game in Who's Afraid of Virginia Woolf and The Boys in the Band. EDWIN MOSES: A Reading of "The Ancient Mariner". JOHN H. RANDALL: Romeo and Juliet in the New World. A Study in James, Wharton, and Fitzgerald "Fay ce que vouldras". JOHN E. SAVESON: Conrad as Moralist in Victory. ROBERT M. STROZIER: Politics, Stoicism, and the Development of Elizabethan Tragedy. LEWIS TURCO: Manoah Bodman: Poet of the Second Awakening.

Volume 9. Amsterdam 1973. 251 p. Hfl. 40.–
THOMAS E. BARDEN: Dryden's Aims in *Amphytryon.* SAMUEL IRVING BELLMAN: Marjorie Kinnan Rawling's Existentialist Nightmare *The Yearling.* SAMUEL IRVING BELLMAN: Writing Literature for Young People. Marjorie Kinnan Rawlings' "Secret River" of the Imagination. F. S. JANZOW: "Philadelphus," A New Essay by De Quincey. JACQUELINE KRUMP: Robert Browning's Palace of Art. ROBERT E. MORSBERGER: The Winning of Barbara Undershaft: Conversion by the Cannon Factory, or "Wot prawce selvytion nah? " DOUGLAS L. PETERSON: Tempest-Tossed Barks and Their Helmsmen in Several of Shakespeare's Plays. STANLEY POSS: Serial Form and Malamud's Schlemihls. SHERYL P. RUTLEDGE: Chaucer's Zodiac of Tales. CONSTANCE RUYS: John Pickering–Merchant Adventurer and Playwright. JAMES H. SIMS: Death in Poe's Poetry: Varia-

tions on a Theme. ROBERT A. SMITH: A Pioneer Black Writer and the Problems of Discrimination and Miscegenation. ALBERT J. SOLOMON: The Sound of Music in "Eveline": A Long Note on a Barrel-Organ. J. L. STYAN: Goldsmith's Comic Skills. ARLINE R. THORN: Shelley's *The Cenci* as Tragedy. E. THORN: James Joyce: Early Imitations of Structural Unity. LEWIS TURCO: The Poetry of Lewis Turco. An Interview by Gregory Fitzgerald and William Heyen.

New Series. Volume 1. Edited by James L. W. West III. Amsterdam 1974. 194 p. Hfl. 40.—

D. W. ROBERTSON, Jr.: Chaucer's Franklin and His Tale. CLARENCE H. MILLER and CARYL K. BERREY: The Structure of Integrity: The Cardinal Virtues in Donne's "Satyre III". F. SAMUEL JANZOW: The English Opium-Eater as Editor. VICTOR A. KRAMER: Premonition of Disaster: An Unpublished Section for Agee's *A Death in the Family*. GEORGE L. GECKLE: Poetic Justice and *Measure for Measure*. RODGER L. TARR: Thomas Carlyle's Growing Radicalism: The Social Context of *The French Revolution*. G. THOMAS TANSELLE: Philip Gaskell's *A New Introduction to Bibliography*. Review Essay. KATHERINE B. TROWER: Elizabeth D. Kirk's *The Dream Thought of Piers Plowman*. Review Essay. JAMES L. WEST III: Matthew J. Bruccoli's *F. Scott Fitzgerald a Descriptive Bibliography*. Review Essay. JAMES E. KIBLER: R. W. Stallman's *Stephen Crane: A Critical Bibliography*. Review. ROBERT P. MILLER: Jonathan Saville's *The Medieval Erotic Alba*. Review.

New Series. Volume 2. **THACKERY. Edited by Peter L. Shillingsburg.** Amsterdam 1974. 359 p. Hfl. 70.—

JOAN STEVENS: *Vanity Fair* and the London Skyline. JANE MILLGATE: History *versus* Fiction: Thackeray's Response to Macaulay. ANTHEA TRODD: Michael Angelo Titmarsh and the Knebworth Apollo. PATRICIA R. SWEENEY: Thackeray's Best Illustrator. JOAN STEVENS: Thackeray's Pictorial Capitals. ANTHONY BURTON: Thackeray's Collaborations with Cruikshank, Doyle, and Walker. JOHN SUTHERLAND: A *Vanity Fair* Mystery: The Delay in Publication. JOHN SUTHERLAND: Thackeray's Notebook for *Henry Esmond*. EDGAR F. HARDEN: The Growth of *The Virginians* as a Serial Novel: Parts 1–9. GERALD C. SORENSEN: Thackeray Texts and Bibliographical Scholarship. PETER L. SHILLINSBURG: Thackeray Texts: A Guide to Inexpensive Editions. RUTH apROBERTS: Thackeray Boom: A Review. JOSEPH E. BAKER: Reading Masterpieces in Isolation: Review. ROBERT A. COLBY and JOHN SUTHERLAND: Thackeray's Manuscripts: A Preliminary Census of Library Locations.

New Series. Volume 3. Edited by James L. W. West III. Amsterdam 1975. 184 p. Hfl. 40.—

SAMUEL J. ROGAL: Hurd's Editorial Criticism of Addison's Grammar and Usage. ROBERT P. MILLER: Constancy Humanized: Trivet's Constance and the Man of Law's Custance. WELDON THORNTON: Structure and Theme in Faulkner's *Go Down, Moses*. JAYNE K. KRIBBS: John Davis: A Man For His Time. STEPHEN E. MEATS: The Responsibilities of an Editor of Correspondence. Review Essay. RODGER L. TARR: Carlyle and Dickens *or* Dickens and Carlyle. Review. CHAUNCEY WOOD: Courtly Lovers: An Unsentimental View. Review.

New Series. Volume 4. Edited by James L. W. West III. Amsterdam 1975. 179 p. Hfl. 40.–
JAMES L. W. WEST III: A Bibliographer's Interview with William Styron. J. TIMOTHY HOBBS: The Doctrine of Fair Use in the Law of Copyright. JUNE STEFFENSEN HAGEN: Tennyson's Revisions of the Last Stanza of "Audley Court". CLIFFORD CHALMERS HUFFMAN: *The Christmas Prince*: University and Popular Drama in the Age of Shakespeare. ROBERT L. OAK-MAN: Textual Editing and the Computer. Review Essay. T.H. HOWARD-HILL: The Bard in Chains: *The Harvard Concordance to Shakespeare.* Review Essay. BRUCE HARKNESS: Conrad Computerized and Concordanced. Review Essay. MIRIAM J. SHILLINGSBURG: A Rose is a Four-Letter Word; or, The Machine Makes Another Concordance. Review Essay. RICHARD H. DAMMERS: Explicit Statement as Art. Review Essay. A. S. G. EDWARDS: Medieval Madness and Medieval Literature. Review Essay. NOEL POLK: Blotner's Faulkner. Review.

New Series. Volume 5–6. **GYASCUTUS. Studies in Antebellum Southern Humorous and Sporting Writing. Edited by James L. W. West III.** Amsterdam 1978.
NOEL POLK: The Blind Bull, Human Nature: Sut Lovingood and the Damned Human Race. HERBERT P. SHIPPEY: William Tappan Thompson as Playwright. LELAND H. COX, Jr.: Porter's Edition of *Instructions to Young Sportsmen.* ALAN GRIBBEN: Mark Twain Reads Longstreet's *Georgia Scenes.* T. B. THORPE's Far West Letters, ed. Leland H. Cox, Jr. An Unknown Tale by GEORGE WASHINGTON HARRIS ed. William Starr. JOHNSON JONES HOOPER's "The 'Frinnolygist' at Fault" ed. James L. W. West III. SOUTH CAROLINA WRITERS in the *Spirit of the Times* ed. Stephen E. Meats. A NEW MOCK SERMON ed. James L. W. West III. ANOTHER NEW MOCK SERMON ed. A. S. Wendel. The PORTER-HOOPER Correspondence ed. Edgar E. Thompson.

New Series. Volume 7. **SANFORD PINSKER: The Languages of Joseph Conrad.** Amsterdam 1978. 87 p. Hfl. 20.–
Table of Contents: Foreword. Introductory Language. The Language of the East. The Language of Narration. The Language of the Sea. The Language of Politics. *Victory* As Afterword.

New Series. Volume 8. **GARLAND CANNON: An Integrated Transformational Grammar of the English Language.** Amsterdam 1978. 315 p. Hfl. 60.–
Table of Contents: Preface. 1) A Child's Acquisition of His First Language. 2) Man's Use of Language. 3) Syntactic Component: Base Rules. 4) Syntactic Component: Lexicon. 5) Syntactic Component: Transformational Rules. 6) Semantic Component. 7) Phonological Component. 8) Man's Understanding of His Language. Appendix: the Sentence-Making Model. Bibliography. Index.

New Series: Volume 9. **GERALD LEVIN: Richardson the Novelist: The Psychological Patterns.** Amsterdam 1978. 172 p. Hfl. 30.–
Table of Contents: Preface. Chapter One. The Problem of Criticism. Chapter Two. "Conflicting Trends" in *Pamela.* Chapter Three. Lovelace's Dream. Chapter Four. The "Family Romance" of *Sir Charles Grandison.* Chapter Five. Richardson's Art. Chapter Six. Richardson and Lawrence: the Rhetoric of Concealment. Appendix. Freud's Theory of Masochism. Bibliography.

New Series: Volume 10. **WILLIAM F. HUTMACHER: Wynkyn de Worde and Chaucer's Canterbury Tales. A Transcription and Collation of the 1498 Edition with Caxton^2 from the General Prologue Through the Knights Tale.** Amsterdam 1978. 224 p. Hfl. 40,–
Table of Contents: Introduction. Wynkyn's Life and Works. Wynkyn De Word's Contribution to Printing. Significance of Wynkyn's *The Canterbury Tales*. Significance of Wynkyn's Order of the Tales. Scheme of the Order of ·*The Canterbury Tales*. Wynkyn's Variants from CX^2. Printer's Errors. Spelling. Omissions in Wynkyn's Edition. Additions in Wynkyn's Edition. Transpositions in Wynkyn's Edition. Miscellaneous Variants in the Reading. Bibliography. Explanation of the Scheme of the Transcription and Recording of the Variants. The Transcription and Collation.

New Series: Volume 11. **WILLIAM R. KLINK: S. N. Behrman: The Major Plays.** Amsterdam 1978. 272 p. Hfl. 45,–
Table of Contents: Introduction. *The Second Man. Brief Moment. Biography. Rain From Heaven. End of Summer. No Time for Comedy. The Talley Method. But For Whom Charlie.* Language. Conclusion. Bibliography.

New Series: Volume 12. **VALERIE BONITA GRAY:** *Invisible Man's* **Literary heritage:** *Benito Cereno* **and** *Moby Dick*. Amsterdam 1978. 145p. Hfl. 30,–
Table of Contents: Democracy: The Politics of "Affirming the Principle" and Celebrating the Individual. The Spectrum of Ambiguity: From Mask Wearing to Shape-shifting. Whiteness or Blackness: Which Casts the Shadow? Melville's and Ellison's Methodology: Bird Imagery and Whale and Circus Lore. Social Protest. Bibliography.

New Series: Volume 13. **VINCENT DIMARCO and LESLIE PERELMAN: The Middle English Letter of Alexander to Aristotle.** Amsterdam 1978. 194p. Hfl. 40,–

New Series: Volume 14. **JOHN W. CRAWFORD: Discourse: Essays on English and American Literature.** Amsterdam 1978. 200p. 40,–
Contents: Chaucer's Use of Sun Imagery. The Fire from Spenser's Dragon: "The Faerie Queene," I.xi. The Changing Renaissance World in Thomas Deloney's Fiction. Shakespeare's Falstaff: A Thrust at Platonism. The Religious Question in *Julius Caesar*. Teaching *Julius Caesar:* A Study in Poetic Persuasion. Shakespeare: A Lesson in Communications. Intuitive Knowledge in *Cymbeline*. White Witchcraft in Tudor-Stuart Drama. Another

Biblical Allusion in *Paradise Lost*. *Absalom and Achitophel;* and Milton's *Paradise Lost*. Asem-Goldsmith's Solution to Timon's Dilemma. Dr. Johnson: A Modern Example of Christian Constancy. A Unifying Element in Tennyson's *Maud*. Arnold's Relevancy to the Twentieth Century. Sophocles' Role in "Dover Beach". Lest We Forget, Lest We Forget: Kipling's Warning to Humanity. The Garden Imagery in *Great Expectations*. "Victorian" Women in *Barchester Towers*. Another Look at "Youth". Forster's "The Road from Colonus". Biblical Influences in *Cry, the Beloved Country*. Huxley's *Island:* A Contemporary *Utopia*. The Generation Gap in Literature. Bred and Bawn in a Briar Patch — Deception in the Making. Success and Failure in the Poetry of Edwin Arlington Robinson. Naturalistic Tendencies in *Spoon River Anthology*. Primitiveness in "The Bravest Boat". Theme of Suffering in "Sonny's Blues". Nabokov's "First Love". The Temper of Romanticism in *Travels with Charley*. Unrecognized Artists in American Literature: Chicano Renaissance.

New Series: Volume 15. **ROBERT F. WILLSON, JR.: Landmarks of Shakespeare Criticism.** Amsterdam 1979. 113p. 25,–
Contents: Introduction. Thomas Rymer: On *Othello* (1692). Nicholas Rowe: Preface (1709-14). Alexander Pope: Preface (1725). Lewis Theobald: Preface (1740). Samuel Johnson: Preface (1765). Richard Farmer: Essay on the Learning of Shakespeare (1767). Gotthold Lessing: On Ghosts (1769). Walter Whiter: On Hell and Night in *Macbeth* (1794). William Richardson: On the Faults of Shakespeare (1797). August Wilhelm von Schlegel: Lecture XXIII. Shakespeare (1809-11). Johann Wolfgang von Goethe: Shakespeare ad Infinitum (1812?). Samuel Taylor Coleridge: On Shakespeare as a Poet (1811-12). William Hazlitt: On Shakespeare and Milton (1818). Thomas de Quincey: On the Knocking at the Gate in *Macbeth* (1823). Thomas Carlyle: The Hero as a Poet (1841). Ivan Turgenev: Hamlet and Don Quixote: the Two Eternal Human Types (1860). Edward Dowden: Shakespeare's Portraiture of Women (1888). Walter Pater: Shakespeare's English Kings (1889). Bernard ten Brink: Shakespeare as a Comic Poet (1895). Richard Moulton: Supernatural Agency in the Moral World of Shakespeare (1903). Leo Tolstoy: Shakespeare and the Drama (1906). J.J. Jusserand: What to Expect of Shakespeare (1911-12). Sigmund Freud: On Lady Macbeth (1916). George Bernard Shaw: On Cutting Shakespear (1919). Edmund Blunden: Shakespeare's Significances (1929). Selected Bibliography.

New Series: Volume 16. **A.H. Qureshi: Edinburgh Review and Poetic Truth.** Amsterdam 1979. 61p. 15,–

New Series: Volume 17. **RAYMOND J.S. GRANT: Cambridge Corpus Christi College 41: The Loricas and the Missal.** Amsterdam 1979. 127p. 30,–
Contents: Chapter I: The Loricas of Corpus 41. Chapter II: Corpus 41 — An 11th-Century English Missal. Appendix: Latin Liturgical material contained in

Editions Rodopi N.V., Keizersgracht 302-304, Amsterdam, the Netherlands.